by Arlet and Sam Wylie

BETWEEN PIETY AND DESIRE

T0116655

Neighborhood Story Project
New Orleans, Louisiana

Other books from the Neighborhood Story Project

Before and After North Dorgenois by Ebony Bolding
The Combination by Ashley Nelson
Palmyra Street by Jana Dennis
What Would the World be Without Women? by Waukesha Jackson

Series Editor: Rachel Breunlin
Graphic Designer: Gareth Breunlin

Let us hear from you. www.neighborhoodstoryproject.org.
Neighborhood Story Project
P.O. Box 19742
New Orleans, LA 70179

DEDICATION

Arlet: I want to dedicate this book to my mama: for raising me the right way, for pushing me to be persistent with my writing. Thank-you for being strong for me and the rest of our family. I pray you'll get the happiness you deserve.

Sam: I want to dedicate this book to my son Samuel David Wylie IV, with much love from your Dad, Samuel David Wylie III. I hope when you get older and read this book, you can look across the room at me and be proud.

ARLET'S ACKNOWLEDGEMENTS

To the Neighborhood Story Project: you helped me use parts of my brain that I didn't know were there.

To Ashley: thanks for being real and always making me laugh. To Jana for being there when I needed someone to talk to. To Kesha for being the first to open up when I thought I couldn't. To Ebony for having no fear when you write. To Ceirod, my co-graduate, congratulations.

To Rachel, for editing interviews and photographs, and for being dedicated when everyone else was too tired and burnt out to work, and for helping inspire me to be a strong woman in this world.

To Abram, for photographs, and for boosting my spirits up when I felt like my writing was going nowhere.

For Steve Gleason, for spending time with the Neighborhood Story Project and for making a commitment to us.

To Lauren and Heather, thank you for helping to transcribe my interviews.

Thanks to Lisa, Martin, Karama and Ariel for giving me stories to write about and for being excited to read my writing. I pray that we stay as close as we are now. You are more than just family, you are the best friends I could ever have.

Sam, Thank you for inviting me to work on the Neighborhood Story Project. You gave me the opportunity to do something I didn't think I could ever do. Even though we've fussed and argued about stories and our book, I've learned a lot about how you think and about our family through your writing. Our family is blessed to have such a good teller of our stories.

To my entire family: thanks for the love and the bonds that we share.

Thank you to Pastor Haynes for always encouraging me and giving me words of wisdom.

To Twine, Mario, and Lemon for lifting my spirits during my teenage years.

To Malcolm, also known as Dooda: keep up the good work in school and one day you will be able to write a book about your life.

To Nedra: continue to stay strong in all you do, and let nothing or no one bring you down.

To Nunnie: I pray you get your education to go forward in life.

To Auntie Lisa: thanks for watching us when my mom didn't have anyone else, and thank you for all your help.

To Grandma: thank you for being strong for the rest of our family.

To Grandma Willemina and Grandpa Harry: thanks for all your support and love.

To my daddy: I love you and thank you for a happy childhood.

To everyone who let me take photos, especially, Kim, Reek, Derek, B, Percy, and Anthony, I hope you like how you look.

To Ms. Gwen, thanks for the interview and allowing me to know you better. I hope your business keeps growing.

And most importantly, to God, thank you for putting me on this earth to share one of my many gifts you've blessed me with.

SAM'S ACKNOWLEDGEMENTS

Thanks to Rachel and Abram for all the help with the interviews and editing and photographs. And thank you Abram for helping me wade through all the bullshit, when you could have just waved to me from the safety of the shore.

The same goes for my sister Ariel, you didn't have to help me out either, but you kept it real, after I told you to leave it alone.

Thank you Mama for raising me right and teaching me enough to have the sense to know how to express myself in writing. I know you've always wanted to write a book, but never got around to it while raising six plus children. I know you're proud now, and I can't wait to read your book when you get the time to do your writing.

I want to thank all the people who've done anything for the Neighborhood Story Project. Even if you were just visiting and gave an opinion or advice, thank you.

Thank you Arlet for partnering with me and making it happen. Thank you for not quitting when times got hard and minds were stressed. You made this book a hundred times better than it would have been if I would have done it alone.

To Martin, keep making your comics and one day I'll be reading your book. Lisa, keep on with your schoolwork, I might need brain surgery one day. Karama, stop stressing out Mama and teach me how to lie: I want my next book to be fiction.

To Dad, I hope your new business turns out all right.

Thank you to my block and all my interviewees: you've played a big part in making this book a lot better.

Jeremy, be cool, stay out of trouble. It's easy to get into and hard to get out of.

To Roy Jones, you're my favorite fighter, and I hope one day to knock you out.

And finally, thank-you Roulette for all the encouragement and all the drama. I pray we both can make it out of this sea together. You know wassup. Let what I did with your ring dwell in your head, and keep keeping me on track. I love you.

TABLE OF CONTENTS

INTRODUCTION

What's up y'all. Welcome to our block, St. Claude Avenue, between Piety and Desire. The Avenue, the main street of the Ninth Ward of New Orleans. The toe of the boot that is Louisiana.

We've been writing this book for a year. We've uncovered the struggles of our family. The process has been sometimes shocking, sometimes scary, sometimes therapeutic and sometimes just plain fun. We've looked at family history, joke-telling, abuse, closeness, and division. We've asked the hard questions that people might not want discussed and taken photos on good and bad days. Our family is very strong, very loving, and very forgiving. We go through hell, but we always get back out.

The book is also about our neighborhood. It discusses what goes on. We have lots of interviews for the curious: we've talked to drug dealers, business-owners, circus punks and people hanging out. We've looked beyond the violence at the real people that the rest of the world judges before they know. And we've taken lots of pictures to help out your imagination.

This is our world, St. Claude, between Piety and Desire Streets, as we see it. Now get ready and prepare yourself, you are entering the Ninth Ward. Welcome.

PART I: GROWING UP INSIDE

Growing up in my house was fun. We always had something to do, and we always stuck together. We went through a lot—dealt with a lot of drama and happiness. Back then was our family's best years, and I miss them a lot. I sometimes wish I could go back for a day to get that feeling back. We're not broken up, but I just don't feel as close to them as I used to.

Honestly, I think everyone's family, if you had one, was closer back when they all were young. Maybe the older people get the less they feel they need their family. But anyway, mine was pretty cool back then. We always had clothes to wear, food to eat, each other for entertainment, and parents who loved and took good care of us. —Sam

ARLET: MY MOTHER

Emelda Antionette Coleman Wylie is my mother's name. She got her first name from her grandmother, which she likes very much because it's an old name. Her maiden name is from her father and last name of course from my father, who she's still married to, to this day.

Her eyes look as if she could see right through you. Her facial expression tells if you should shut up, talk, or when she doesn't feel like being bothered. Whenever someone meets her, they say how much of a good person she is. They compliment us and tell her how respectable we are and say things like, "You have some good kids."

When I was old enough to realize that she worked so hard to raise us the right way, I admired that. When I was little my mother always asked her children—Ariel, the oldest; Sam, named after my dad; Arlet, myself; Martin, inspired by Martin Luther King; Lisa, named after my aunt; and Karama, who has the best name of all—"What are you going to be when you grow up?" We would reply in small high pitched voices, "Something great." This meant no matter what you do be the best. If it's a garbage man—be the best.

In the morning she irons all our uniforms and when we get home we have to take our uniforms off and put them on the hangers ready to wear the next

day. Then we put on play clothes and watch TV for awhile and then do our homework. When I was little, homework was what I hated to do; it was so hard for me to finish. My worst subjects were reading and spelling. If I had trouble with a word, my mom would make me sound it out. If I still didn't get it and I got it wrong a third time I'd get a whuppin. At school my mother didn't play with us when it came down to our work and disrespecting our teachers. We all knew that, and so the only time she came to school was for a play, a parent-teacher conference, or an award ceremony we had.

For Easter, the girls would get all dressed up in our pretty white dresses with laced socks made by my mother and shiny black shoes. The boys wore their fresh crisp white button down shirts, long white socks, and brand new church shoes. My mom would press all the girls' hair the night before and put them in Shirley Temple curls with white ribbons.

She would cut Karama and Sam's hair in a low fade with a lining. She wouldn't cut Martin's hair because he has dreds.

I would do anything for my mama, but I feel whatever I do won't be enough. Not for her but for me. She would appreciate whatever we gave her even if it were something as simple as a homemade card. She's a very appreciative person mainly because she's used to the majority of the time giving and not receiving. My mother is the type of person if you need help she'll help, not worrying about if you're going to pay her back in some way. A number of family members have stayed with us on my mother's side but mostly on my father's side. She never asked them to help her financially at all or even watch us while she was gone.

Someone's child was always there. Almost every summer my cousins from my dad's side would come over and stay with us. It seemed as if they were closer to my mama than my dad. I don't know how she did it. Ariel was six, Sam five, myself four, Martin three, Lisa two, and Karama only one. She also had my cousins Victor, Victoria, Leroy, Tasha, Nedra, and sometimes Tresea. Just her own children were a lot, plus an extra four and sometimes more. My mama practically raised my cousin Katie from the time she was three years old—the same age with my youngest brother Karama. My mom taught her, cared for her, as if she was conceived out of her womb. When my mama bought us clothes, Katie got clothes, when we got shoes, Katie got shoes. She was like another little sister to me and the rest of my siblings.

I didn't realize all the trials and tribulations my mother had to go through for us. Even though she was feeling bad, she still cooked, washed the dishes, and cleaned up after us. She was still strong enough to comfort us when we had a bad day. Even though she was hurt and felt like giving up she pushed herself to go and stay strong for us.

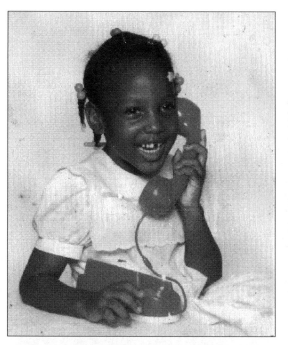

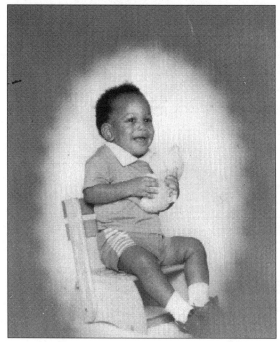

ARLET:
INTERVIEW WITH MOM, PART 1

We grew up on a street that didn't feel much like a neighborhood and I wondered what it was like for my mom growing up. What did she do for fun and was her mom as strict on her as she is on us, or does she give us more lee way than we knew. She's always been independent and in this interview, I learned how she came to be this way.

Emelda: My grandmother and my grandfather were from Wallace, Louisiana and they spoke Creole when they first came to New Orleans. I remember her practicing how to speak like people in New Orleans, because they had like a French accent when they spoke. Some of the original people still do, not so much the people that are coming up now. I remember her telling me she worked on trying to lose that.

From what I can remember, they moved to the uptown area around the Brown Derby on First Street. Everything was uptown until she separated from my grandfather. I don't know how old my mom was when they separated, but my grandmother moved in the Desire Projects around 1958.

The area was nice. Every apartment complex had hedges around it. It had trees. There wasn't a lot of crime in that area and it was affordable. I never asked her why, but I'm assuming that's why she chose that area, because at the time it was new. It had only been up maybe a year or two. The whole building where my grandmother lived was single-mothers. But most of the court, in the Desire, it was family housing. It wasn't unwed mothers like it is now. You were single by divorce, or single by death— it was family oriented.

DESIRE

Arlet: Okay, mom, what was it like growing up?

E: Up until the first grade, most of the time I was with my grandmother. I would go home on weekends. I wasn't spoiled, but I was the first grandchild, so everybody made out over me and they would always tell me I was this amazing baby. My mom had a lot of high expectations for me.

Growing up, I was just everybody's child for some reason. Everybody basically took to me. Or I took to everybody. I was always around my grandmother, my older cousins and my aunts. Those were the people that I talked to. I was this old person, but I was a child, you know?

They would talk like a grownup around me. I was never the child that had to go in the back unless my mama was home. I was always the child in adult company. And I learned a lot from them, and they always made me feel special because the rest of the children weren't allowed. I guess they acted so much like children, and I didn't. I would basically keep quiet and listen to the conversation and just fall out laughing at stuff that they would say.

As I got older, I would become more and more shy. I didn't have a lot of friends. I hated going to school because kids were cruel. We were never allowed to look like everybody else. My mom would make my clothes sometimes. To me, looking back at it, I was always dressed. Every year, I knew I was going to get penny loafers with brand new pennies in them and bobbie socks. I didn't have chemicals in my hair; I didn't have a perm. My mom wasn't big on combing hair [and] my grandmother didn't know how, so my hairstyle every day was three plaits and one ribbon.

I don't think I was the type of kid that made an impression on anybody. I didn't think anything about it at the time, but my whole report card would be all E's—even in behavior. Some mornings I hated to go to school because my grandmother used to feed me coffee and butter and bread in the morning. It was strong, strong coffee. I'd be so full that when I would get to school I would smell the school lunch and just be sick to my stomach.

I don't remember a lot of the stuff about living in the projects because we weren't allowed to go outside and mingle when I lived at my grandmother's house. Only when my grandmother went out, and she watched us, would we play. Right across the court was a good friend of my grandmother's. We could play with them, and we could play with the people that lived next door to my grandmother. And that was it. And um, my aunt basically, played every game with us. She was real strict. And we would have to ask, "Ma, can I look out the window?" And we watched all the children play.

It's a pattern in our family. You basically had no friends because your family members were your friends. I remember we would always have jump rope, football, basketball, bike—things to occupy our minds. We would play a lot of board games just with each other. We didn't have a lot of outside friends, and we didn't miss it because [there were] so many of us.

Dancing was a big part of growing up in the projects. Everybody danced. It was just a way of life. If you didn't dance, it was like, "You a nerd." We danced in the court. We danced at parties. In the projects, it was like every Friday was a party at my grandmother's house, or at her sister's house, because she lived in the projects too. Every Friday they would drink beer. I remember drinking beer all my life.

RESPONSIBILITY

My parents separated when I was three. That marriage didn't last long at all. I remember a fight that my mom and dad had. I remember how the kitchen table looked. I remember how the chairs looked. I had to be really little because I remember getting my youngest sister and going under the table. They were really fighting. They weren't just arguing, they were fighting, and that was my first time seeing that. I remember my mom telling my dad to stop: "Stop, look at my babies."

It's sad, but that's the only recollection I have of my mom and dad ever being together. The thing about it is, my dad never stopped being a part of our life. I remember when I was about seven or eight, they went to get a divorce and he was trying to get custody of us. My mama was crying because she couldn't afford an attorney and he had one and was trying to get us. I remember that much.

A: So how did she wind up keeping y'all?

E: He didn't win the custody. I don't know why he didn't win. I remember when he went off to the army. When he came home, he didn't think we would remember him. I was at my grandmother's house, and somebody was saying, "Harry coming. Harry out there." He had on the army outfit, and he must of left when we were babies because he didn't think my sister Lisa, who was a baby in arms would remember him. He was so surprised he started crying because she ran up to him.

My mom was a nurse and she worked 3 – 11. When we were at school, she was at home. Sometimes I remember being hungry – not destitute, starving hungry, but I remember being hungry sometimes, because my mom would be at work. We didn't have a lot, but I really didn't know that we were poor. She was an excellent cook. I mean, real good cook.

I remember having a lot of structure and a lot of order. When we got older, we moved out on Desire Street [and] then we moved back again when I was in fifth grade. That's when I started all the cooking—I mean, full meals— and the watching the children and fighting. I remember fighting for my brothers. I don't know why I would fight if somebody picked on them, or tried to take anything from them. We would shoot marbles. I played all the boy games and I played all the girl games. I would play football with them, and help them learn how to ride bikes.

I hated the responsibility because nobody else had to clean up. Nobody else knew how but me. My mom had this king sized bed when we lived in the projects. She had a velvet spread, and it was so heavy. She would teach me how to make up the bed, and I didn't make up the bed exactly like she made up the bed, she stripped the whole bed off and I had to start all over.

I learned how to mop—oh, I'll never forget that. We always got these industrial mops, and they were real heavy. I used to be angry when I had to clean up because it just was too much. If I didn't do it right, she would dump the whole mop bucket on the floor. "You left this spot. Look how you got this smudge!" I had to be perfect and I always had to know better. I remember that. "You should know better! You're too old for this and you're too old for that."

Sam: You think that effected how you are now? If it did, do you think it made you be a better person?

A: Because a lot of stuff you're saying you do us the same thing. You not as strict as that, but, a lot of that stuff, like, "You know better than that"' or "You know how to do it."

E: Well, the difference is you didn't start off as little as I was.

A: I know that

E: In my heart, I felt like my mom should have been more like a mom. I understood that she worked but I remember all the time thinking, "These aren't my children."

A: She was trying to take some of that load off herself.

E: Yeah. Overall, I think it made me stronger. It didn't kill me. It taught me maturity, but at the same time, it didn't allow me to be free as a child.

SAM: STORY ABOUT MY DAD

Ever since I could walk and talk and had an understanding of the world around me, my dad and I were close. I used to feel so safe and protected and entertained by anything he did— especially when he would ask me to help. Back then anything we did together was priceless and I wouldn't have traded those moments for anything.

I loved my dad so much I think my mother was jealous. When I was in pre K, if my mother had brought me to class, I would try to rush her out the door and wouldn't stop pushing until she was gone. If my dad brought me, I used to holler and scream and clinch tight to one of his legs—so tight that if I were to grip any harder you'd have to pry me off with a crowbar.

My dad moved to the United States from Belize with his parents when he was twelve years old. His daddy opened up a car repair shop near the Florida Projects in the Ninth Ward and the family lived above it. Once his parents were set up, other relatives started moving into their house, too. They all lived in that house together until they started getting their own house. After he graduated from Carver, he did every kind of hard work there is. He had another life before he was with my mama. He had other children.

My dad is tall with a big stomach. When he sits down he puts his hands on top of his belly like an armrest, or like he's pregnant. He used to be good looking when he was younger, but now he looks old. He dyes his hair to cover up the grey. He wears Muslim hats that he makes himself. He says he wants to convert to Islam, but has never joined up with the religion. He wears leather jackets, carries a pool stick wherever he goes, and finds his clothes in thrift stores. When his pants get too small, he'll cut them into shorts and use the other material to make another hat or something.

My dad is really good with his hands. Besides hats, he makes canes out of wood that he finds. Some are normal with just a handle. On other ones he carves dice, footballs, alligators, and a few times a penis that's positioned to hold in your hand while you are walking down the street. When we were little, he used to make us slingshots out of wood that he found, too. He gave us a bag of beans and told us to shoot at some birds.

My dad's a hustler. He's done just about every hard working kind of job. He owns a mechanic shop in the Ninth Ward and used to run a barroom below our house. On his free time, he taught himself how to be a magician by reading books and watching tapes. Now people pay him to do birthday parties. He can make animals disappear—cats, puppies, and special birds. He keeps buying white doves to use in his tricks and they never make it more than a year. He used to use rabbits as well, but decided he'd rather eat them.

He recruits us to cook as well. I cut up potatoes, crack eggs, clean and fry fish. He doesn't cook that often, but when he does it's a lot. He'll have five pots going at the same tine. He'll cook the rice and the red beans in the pot together and it comes out dry, dry, dry. In another pot he'll have the meat with gravy and ox tails and turkey necks. He'll have bread pudding in the oven. He uses all the pots and pans and my mama gets mad because he don't wash nothing up.

Sometimes he'd just call us into the kitchen and tell us to watch, "You need to pay attention to what I'm doin. Nobody's gonna be cookin for y'all when y'all get older. Y'all are gonna be cookin for y'allself." He's quiet; he don't say nothing except hum a song to himself. When the food finished, he don't say nothing. He'll make himself a plate and go into his room. He cooks so much food, we have almost a week of leftovers.

Everything he cooks with, it's got to have his peppers. He used to grow them himself, but, like the doves, they kept dying. I think he might roll past people's houses and pick a couple out of their yards or something. He takes them and puts them in jars of plain vinegar with a bunch of vegetables—celery, carrots, onions, and cauliflower, cucumbers— and the peppers. It takes a couple months before he opens them up again and when he does it's spiiiicy! He'll eat the vegetables just like that. It's not surprising cuz he pops habanero peppers in his mouth like it's candy.

He makes boxes that he uses to make people disappear or cut them in half. One time, when he was test running the disappearing box, he asked me to be his assistant. My brothers and sisters gathered in his room for the performance. It was a fairly regular event. I stepped into the black box and he closed the door and put a black sheet around it. I felt the box spin around a few times and I started to get scared. I thought maybe I would disappear for real. I couldn't see anything. I heard the hinges squeaking as he opened the door and heard him say, "Ta Da!" but I was still in the box. I heard my siblings say, 'Where Sam at? Where Sam at?" I didn't know either. I thought when I stepped out of the box, I might be on another planet. He seemed to have that kind of power.

ARLET: STRICT

We're little only allowed
two cookies.

In the morning
we had a balanced meal:
grits, eggs,
sausage, biscuits
or pancakes, eggs,
& those lil pork links.
At lunch we ate
hamburgers, fries,
and Kool-aid
or tuna fish sandwiches.
For dinner we got
a half smothered steak,
mashed potatoes, and peas,
meatballs and spaghetti,
with corn and Kool-aid.

Everything we did was timed.
We were programmed to wake up
at 8 o'clock.
A few times we rode our bikes
in the parking lot for two hours.
After it got dark, we had quiet time.
Baths were scheduled
In order to be in bed
for eight o'clock.

SAM: ARIEL

All my life I've looked up to my older sister Ariel. She probably never noticed, but I've always wanted to be like her. I've always wanted to do the things she did. Even if it meant following in her footsteps when she was doing wrong, I looked at it like, "She did so I want to do it too."

My sister is multi-talented. It's like she dished out talents to the rest of us. Mainly she's a singer but she can dance a little like my sister Arlet. She can play a little piano just like me. She can draw a little like Martin. Like Lisa, she has that I don't care and is very smart attitude. Like Karama, she can lie. Well, not as much, but she can lie.

Ariel was our second mother. I mean, really really a mother to us. When I was a baby I used to wake up in the middle of the night or early in the morning crying. That was normal for my age—babies do that, it's natural. But it wasn't natural when Ariel, only one year older than me, used to wake up too and take her bottle out of her mouth and put it in mine. Ariel's not afraid of anyone anytime. She could fight anyone who stands in front of her, regardless of what size you are. She doesn't care. In elementary school, we always stuck together and Ariel was protector of the flock. When boys wanted to fight me, Ariel had my back. She even fought for me at times. She never let anyone hurt her family.

My sister used to make things in the kitchen and sell them to us. She used to take pieces of aluminum and smear peanut butter and raisins on top of the foil. She sold it by the piece for 15 cents. We used to search around the house for any loose change we could find and try to buy some (as if we couldn't make some ourselves). It used to be so much fun until my mother found out and closed shop. If I had three wishes one would be to win the power ball and move away. The second would be to win the power ball again and my third would be to go back about eleven years in time and spend a day or two back when Ariel used to make peanut butter, raisin, sprinkled foils.

We used to fuss and almost fight when we were younger over stupid stuff like when we had to wash dishes. She used to chase me with a knife around the kitchen if I didn't cooperate. That used to be somewhat fun but mostly scary. The one and only thing I

didn't like was her vicious headlock. Once you're in it, you can't get out. Whenever we played wrestling, it was in our best interest to try to avoid that headlock. To this day, I couldn't get out of it if I tried.

Ariel might not have been able to show me how to be a man, but she taught me a lot about life: how to get a job, how to go about getting checked for STDs, how listening to the radio while studying can help me learn better, everything I know about preventing pregnancy and safe sex, how to talk to a girl, just about, or almost everything I know. To be honest, I would listen to her before I listen to my own parents.

Whenever I think about what she used to do for me, I feel bad. I feel bad because I never did any of those things for her. I can't recall ever saying thank-you. She's gone now, in the Air Force. Quite naturally that's what I plan on doing after I graduate. Just like her. I'm eighteen now and still follow in my big sister's shoes, or at least I'm trying to.

My sister feels that the Air Force was the best choice for her since she didn't want to go to college. She feels that this was a good chance to get physically fit then earn a lot of money. She also says it's a good opportunity to get away from family and all the drama in it. Basically, I just want to go because she went. There are other reasons, though. I also feel that it is a good opportunity to earn money to

support my son. Yes, I have a son. He's eighteen months. Not saying I don't love my son with all my heart, but if I had listened to my sister, he wouldn't be here now. I know I'm young, but there couldn't have been another time I could feel so proud about disobeying my sister. She always told me to protect myself, but seeing what a blessing he is to me, I'm glad I didn't.

ARLET: CHILDHOOD GAMES

My dad had children before he had us. He really wasn't there for them like he wanted and needed to be because of his relationship with his children's mothers and also because he wanted to live his life how he wanted. Seeing all the things that he did wrong and realizing that he didn't raise his other children and they didn't turn out to be successful people made him imagine what he would do right with his other children. I think being with my mom as we grew up he thought that would help him to be a better father. Having a man's influence on our life and a man's discipline made us better. All together I think having my parents' love made us not go other places for it.

My sisters, brother, and I played and had fun in odd ways. My dad was always gone off shore so he never knew what we were doing. We took my dad's underwear and used it to clean out the garbage can with bleach and dish washing liquid and fill it with water (which, by the way, was very big because we had a big family). We took the trashcan and put it on our back porch in front of a Pac-man machine and filled it up with water. We had an unexplainable amount of fun jumping from the machine into the trashcan. When we got tired, we'd go inside, making a mess on the kitchen floor, and then look for a big towel to dry off. If we couldn't find enough towels, we bundled up in pairs in one towel.

Most days my oldest sister and I dressed up in our bathing suits, got on top of the dresser and danced in front of the mirror. It was like a hobby changing clothes and looking in the mirror to see how I looked. My little sister was so little and cute, she never really had clothes on at all. A lot of the time we would all get in the tub together. Two people take a bar of soap and scrub the back rim, sides, and bottom of the tub. Completely undressed, we started sliding like we were on a real water slide in a water park or something. To make it more interesting, we sometimes cut on the shower.

In my parents room was a hammock. Yes, a hammock that's supposed to be outside, but because my dad is from Belize he has it inside. The hammock was big, stitched with a thick material handmade by my dad. I guess he would have put it outside, but we didn't have a real back yard, just a porch because we lived on top of the store. Maybe it was because he wanted to share his culture with us. Swinging in the hammock is what we loved to do and one day we made up a game called "Slingshot." Each of us, one at a time, would get in the hammock and everybody else pulled the hammock all the way to the back and let go. As soon as they let go the person in the hammock flew in the air and landed on the bed.

On our back porch was a 4 or 5 foot playhouse that could hold all six of us. My daddy made it by hand. The playhouse was used for so many different things: a club house where only certain people could get in, a candy lady where Ariel and me used to sell peanut butter and raisins on aluminum foil for a nickel, and tea parties. We set up this play tea set that my parents bought the girls for Christmas. We used the play dishes for real—mostly pouring enough Kool aid in the cup for a sip. Afterwards, Ariel pretended that she was washing and putting the dishes up.

Almost everyday we would play hide and seek. There was a rhyme or trick we said that made it easy

to tell who was "it." Ariel was always the one who started it off. No one had a problem with it because we thought the oldest was always leading. Ariel said, "Put your hand in a cookie jar, one for me." Whoever put in a hand for her, they were "it." We hid in a tub, in the kitchen cabinet, in our toy box, and also in the closet, using the clothes as camouflage.

These games are very precious to me because of the uniqueness, oddity, and originality of them. That is why I wanted to share them with the world.

ARLET: BURNED

We were just coming in from school and my mama said she wanted to cook. Sam volunteered to light the stove, but couldn't get it lit and accidentally left the gas on when he went to the bathroom to get something. I walked into the kitchen to see if he got the oven working and I saw my daddy's head in the bottom of the oven trying to light the pilot.

Before Sam could warn him, a big ball of fire exploded in my dad's face. I was in awe and thought maybe his face had blown up. As he rose to his feet, he looked like a mad man. The kitchen smelled of burnt hair and smoke. He had so much pride he wanted to seem like he wasn't hurting. My mama was not making it any better by saying, "Aw Sam, what happened?" I wanted so bad to say, "Sam blew his face up."

ARLET: D & D FOOD STORE

As long as I can remember I lived on top of D&D Food Store. As a little girl, the store was always in my memory. I always thought being on top of a store I could go down when I wanted candy, chips, pickles, or a juice, but of course it didn't work that way. Instead, we would be buy necessities we needed like bread, an onion, ham, or luncheon meat. Every now and then, we would buy cigarettes for my mother, but first she would call the store to let them know we were coming.

My parents wouldn't let us go downstairs by ourselves. We always went in pairs. I wasn't scared or intimidated by the people in the store or the Asian family that ran it because I felt that my family owned the building. It gave me a sense of security. Inside, there were all kinds of video games that, at the time, were twenty-five cents. When someone was cooking the entire store smelled of hot fried chicken, French fries, egg rolls, and all other types of greasy food. Sometimes we played with the Asian family's kids on our porch. I distinctly remember a girl about two years older than me named Kim. We would play hide and seek, dig up worms, and make mud pies.

At the beginning of my teenage years, another Asian family took over the store. They used to rush us by saying things like, "Hurry up and buy." Or just look at us as if we were going to steal something. It

never happened to any of us, but I think they used to argue with a lot of people who would come in and out of their store. They might have done this because they were new to black people and also, what they thought they knew about us. Evidently, they didn't have to stress the NO LOITERING policy because no one hung out there except for the teenage boys playing Pac Man and Street Fighter. My parents would stop by to pick up our mail.

Everything stayed the same until my mom finally got a job. Before then my mother was a stay at home mom. Then when I was six years old my mother went back to school because she wanted her own money and didn't like to be dependent on my father. Later she began to do student teaching and she got her first real job teaching at Locket Elementary School. Her paychecks came in the mail. One day, the Asian family didn't open the store when my mother was waiting for her check. My mother was furious. Right then she made up her mind that the mail would stop going to the store. On the door was a mail slot and words that spelled out "Put 3316 St. Claude Mail Here."

The store finally opened and my mother told them to take the sign down because she had some impor-

tant mail being sent to our house and we weren't getting it because the store was closed. They refused. My mother began tearing the sign down anyway. The Asian lady, short and a little heavy-set, began shouting in a loud voice for my mother to stop but she wasn't paying attention. The lady approached my mother and touched her on the shoulders. My mother immediately turned around and hit the lady so hard in the mouth her tooth hung. The lady didn't fight back. She just yelled, "Go call the police!" repeatedly. My mother yelled back in rage, "You rent, I own! Remember that!"

The police came. Hearing what had happened before he got there, the officer automatically wanted to bring my mother to jail. There was a video camera watching the whole thing and that's what saved her. When they realized that the lady touched her first they were both summoned to court. The other lady wanted to press charges. When we arrived at court we later found out all charges were dropped.

Years later, another Asian family moved in and they were really nice. I guess it was after they got to know us. There's an Asian man named Nick that works in the store and is just a cool person. He's a man in his mid 30s. He's a more easy going person, where not too much bothers him. Nick lets people eat their food in the store. He talks to the boys in my neighborhood like he's one of us. If one of the boys would say, "Nick, stupid bitch," he'll say, "Fuck you," and they wouldn't think anything of it. Most of the time I'll go into the store and he'll tell people I'm his girlfriend. If he hasn't seen me in a while he'll say something like, "Where you been, baby?" I don't feel uncomfortable because I know he's just playing.

The store has changed a lot. Now there's a big iron gate just before you walk in. It reminds me of being in jail. There are no games anymore. The whole store is totally remodeled. The other Asian family wasn't able to get along with people because they were too uptight. But for this family, being around people from another culture and understanding them better made it easier to get along.

SAM: RIBBED

When I was young, I was afraid to go outside by myself when there were a lot of older people around. I never told anyone, but sometimes they picked with me. They blocked the store so I couldn't get in and made fun of me—talking about my head or what I had on, or anything that came to their minds. I never said anything to them because they were bigger than me and way older. It would have only made matters worse. Then people would look at me like, "Oh, that boy scary. All he do is tell on people." And then people would really mess with me.

I never told my family because I didn't want them to get into anything with any of them. My family is crazy over their relatives. All you have to do is tell them one time, and they'd be ready to kill somebody. I'm glad I didn't pick up that mentality, because a lot of people would have been severely hurt a long time ago.

Sometimes I still over hear little kids getting ribbed by the older guys. They'll say, "Oh, look at this lil big head bitch. Always beggin for money," or "Damn, that lil nigga skinny," or "Damn, that lil nigga dirty. Say boy, why ya mama don't feed you?" I'll say, "Hey cuz, leave that lil dude alone, he bout to cry." Usually they'll be like, "All right," and stop.

As I grew older, I didn't have to live in fear of going outside alone, but I still had to watch for people who might want to harm me. When I was small, I didn't understand that these people were just playing around with me. Teenagers wouldn't try to physically hurt me—it's all just a stunt in front of their friends. The older you are, things get a little more complex. Now they're testing your heart—basically pushing up a fight.

SAM: BELIZE

I've always wondered what it would be like in Belize. I've always imagined dirt roads and palm trees and coconut trees everywhere. I thought people there walked around bare foot all the time and had an accent so strong, you could never make out what they were saying.

Ariel went to Belize with my dad when I was nine and she came back with their accent. I thought it was cool to sound like that, and that really made me want to visit there! I finally got my chance to go, but the trip took longer than I expected, three days or longer. We drove the whole, long, boring way, my younger brother Martin, my younger sister Arlet, my mom and my dad.

When we got there it was nothing like I expected it to be, except for the fact that I could hardly understand anyone. My father's mom talks like that, and I understand her. But these people spoke a little more swiftly and I couldn't catch on completely. There were no dirt roads or palm trees. Most of it looked like New Orleans. The difference was that the majority of the people in Belize grew plants and trees or fruit and vegetables, none for decoration, all for food. Their neighborhood streets could be twins to New Orleans streets. And their stores look exactly the same.

Anyway when I first got there I was like, "Wow, I'm in Belize, so this is what it looks like." I wondered what my relatives down here would be like. Would they like us? Will they accept us? Will we be friends and get along?

It turned out being cool. Nobody was shy or afraid to talk to us. They all greeted us open armed, from the youngest to the oldest. They just started kicking off all types of questions and telling us about themselves. They asked our age and told theirs. They asked if we understood what they were saying. They even told us their races. There were some black, Indian, mixed Indian and black, even white. And my dad isn't really too fond of white people. He always talked about how they used to treat us, but let them talk Creole, and they'll be best friends.

After talking and listening to them for a while, I felt comfortable. And the next day was better, we were well rested and energized with plans to have as much fun as possible. And that's just what we did. We played "it" with my little cousins and hide and seek and Frisbee. We practically stayed in the store to buy Ideal, a Belizean freeze pop. The only difference is that they make theirs with milk and juice. Some of it is just basically ice cream in a pack.

We had a lot of fun, especially when we went to one of their islands. That was the most beautiful piece of earth I had ever seen. There was a partly nude beach that we went to with one of my cousins. The women there didn't wear any tops. But the place was so pretty that I paid them hardly no attention. The water was sky blue and the fish were colorful. The sand was smooth and clean with tall coconut trees growing from it. There was a bar right next to the trees, in case you got thirsty. There were restaurants all over and fishing equipment stores. Just about everything you could name was there. Jet skis, boat rides, canoeing, parasailing, water skiing, everything, even stores for scuba diving. It's definitely a place you would want to take your husband or wife on a honeymoon. It's not even that expensive. Fifty cents of our money is one of their dollars, so you don't have to worry about spending an arm and a leg.

We stayed out there in a hotel for about two days, then went back. And man did I hate to leave. We still had fun, but not as much there.

After two weeks, we packed up and went to the airport and flew to California and from there, home. I was so hurt when I got on the plane. I wanted to cry so badly because I knew when I got home, everything would be different. Meaning no more beach, no more swimming, no more peace, no more fun. It was back to St. Claude Ave. Our time to get away from it all was over. Back from paradise, returning to mayhem.

PART II: LOOKING OUTSIDE

We never went outside—staying to ourselves was the best thing for us, or so my mom thought. She didn't want us conversating with the riffraff, or "street trash," as she called them. "Thugs" was also another word she used frequently.

Our block of St. Claude is known as a hustle spot. A lot of people see these young teenage boys who hang outside as having no lives, no jobs, no morals and no family values. I thought so, too, until I got to be a teenager and started hanging outside on my balcony.

I went outside when I was bored or just tired of watching TV all day. Maybe my mama or daddy made me mad and I knew if I stayed inside I'd be cantankerous. I went outside to clear my head, but as I spent more time on my balcony I also started to get to know the guys that I had always seen growing up, but never knew personally.

As I learned more about them, I started to realize that the stereotypes were not all true. They are more complex than that. Over time, I became more curious to know what's the word on the street. I liked to listen to their conversations. I knew if I sat outside, I was going to laugh.

Sometimes when I'm having a really good time talking to some of the guys it's hard to remember that they are caught up in a lifestyle that's dangerous. One day they could be clowning and the next day they could be killed. —Arlet

SAM:
VIOLENCE IN THE NEIGHBORHOOD

Whether it's day or night, it's always a bad idea to hang around my block. There have been a lot of times when there's been violence and people have been hurt or even killed.

I always thought my block of St. Claude Avenue between Piety and Desire was backwards—like it doesn't belong where it is. There's a hospital, a few clinics, a church, a children's daycare, and a bunch of stores all packed in one spot. You'd think it would be a good spot to live. Well, it's not. Yes, it has advantages, but the disadvantages completely outweigh them.

Have you ever been awakened out of your sleep because of gunshots or the sound of someone trying to break into your house? I have. I was young, too—about 9 or 10. It was right before I went to sleep and I'll never forget it. I was just sitting in my bed, listening to my sister's radio when I heard two boys fussing over drugs and money. I can't remember every word they said, but the last thing I heard was, "All right, wait 'til I get back."

I peeked out my window but no one was there; all I saw were cars passing by. Being tired, I laid down in my bed and went to sleep. Just as I drifted off, I heard those loud gunshots. Immediately, I remembered what my parents told me to do. I got on the floor and stayed there until my dad said it was okay to get up. My heart was beating fast and I was breathing hard. I thought a bullet was going to hit me through the wall or window. From then on I never liked to look out of that window.

Not long ago, there was a shooting on the corner of St. Claude and Desire. It escalated from a fight about one month prior to the shooting. A boy named Lemon was jumped. He never talked much and always had a serious look on his face. His clothes were always clean, no matter what he wore—usually jeans, a white t-shirt and a different pair of shoes every day of the week. He didn't seem like a troublemaker but he must have gotten into some kind of trouble. About a month went by and it seemed like nothing else was going to happen, but I was wrong. As soon as I thought it was officially over, Lemon was shot.

Some days—almost everyday—I imagine what it would be like if I could win the power-ball and move away from that environment. Sometimes I wish I could just find a suitcase full of hundred dollar bills. I'd buy a big house in the country where the next neighbor is a half a mile away. I'd have a big pool in my backyard and a two-car garage built on the side of my house. It would be just me, my wife, and two or three kids. That would be the perfect life for me. My money would be in the bank and half invested in Wal-Mart stores.

Then I come back to my senses and see that's a long way from 3316 St. Claude Avenue. It would be all up to a game of luck or working really hard for years and years. I know my fantasy is possible, but it's definitely not probable.

SAM:
INTERVIEW WITH AN "AVON SELLER"

My neighborhood is one big money making spot. It's coming in from everywhere, and not just the legal businesses. There are hustlers everywhere. One thing about around there is that nobody, and I mean nobody, accepts being broke.

We make money the best way we can, whether it's legal or illegal. We have a lot of different ways to make money. We have it all: there are doctors, teachers, store owners, repair shops, carpenters and then there are drug dealers, prostitutes, pimps, bootleggers, and people selling stuff they stole.

My thing is, we all know them by what they do, but not as people. We especially stereotype hustlers as violent and ignorant, but honestly, some of them are just like normal people trying to make a living.

Abram and I interviewed one of them, whose name will remain anonymous for personal reasons, and he had a whole lot to say. He's fifteen years old, and to me, seems like he's confused subconsciously on whether to be hard, or tough, and just a kid. One minute he's talking about laughing and having fun with his friends, and the next he talks about "whopping people," or hitting people, and selling "Avon" for money.

Sam: Why you be around here?

Avon Seller: Basically to chill; to chill with the fellas. We have fun ribbin. Some people be smokin. I don't smoke, myself, you know.

S: How long you been around here?

AS: About fifteen years.

S: All your life?

AS: Yeah.

SELLING AVON

S: How do you feel about the neighborhood?

AS: It's nice, I'm lovin it. You sit right down on that porch right here, and all of us, we be about—all of us together be about twenty people like right here. I'm out here 24/7. Just ask one of my co-workers.

S: What you do for money?

AS: Uh, I sell Avon.

S: Are you jokin?

AS: Yeah.

S: You got co-workers?

AS: Yeah, I got a few co-workers. My son Buzzle, my son Jizzle, a lot of them are incarcerated right now. See, we got my son—I think they're on they lunch break, man, today. They probably on they lunch break or something like that. So what else you want to ask me?

S: Does Avon smell good?

AS: Ooh, yes indeed, yes indeed. See I got that little white cream, you dig, the hard cream like.

And I add two for ten on that. You heard me, y'all just holler at me. On St. Claude you want that three for ten, the herbs—like the incense—the fire herbs, you dig. That lime green—three for ten dollars at me. Just ask for Foots.

BUSINESS PHILOSOPHY

S: Would you change anything about your set or whatever?

AS: Everything would be to me. For me.

S: Whaa?

AS: Yeah, the business and everything.

Abram: What would you do with it? Would you keep it all the same?

AS: No, increase it. I'd pump it.

S: Like what you mean?

AS: I'd have the money goin up.

S: How you plan on doin that?

AS: Easy, I'm a salesman.

S: So you're gonna sell something at the hospital?

AS: Everything. Whatever I can put on the streets in a day.

S: At the day center, too?

AS: Yeah, everything. I'll sell to little children, it don't matter.

S: To little kids, dawg?

AS: Somebody want to buy em, holla at me.

VIOLENCE

S: You get along with your people?

AS: I don't ever get into it with nobody, to be honest. We're like family around here. I don't know how to say it, you know sometimes you get into it, but as a group united together, we family. The only time I get into it is like if one of my friends get into it.

S: Yeah, if something go down with one of y'all, everybody go down?

AS: Yeah, everybody, bro.

S: You ever had a time like that?

AS: Yeah all the time. We just beat up a rock head the other day.

S: Why?

AS: I don't know, bored. You see me, and my little bro, Butter, we're like the youngest ones around here so we mostly be doin all the crazy stuff. All the older fellas, they just be chillin.

A: What's some of the crazy stuff that you feel like telling us about?

AS: Whack people. I don't rib like we be talking about, just whack people in the jaw and keep goin.

S: Just cuz?

AS: I don't know, it just comes out.

A: And do you do it to people in your clique or people not in your clique?

AS: Whoever. I don't play with all them. Not people that be with us a lot, you know, but other people we hit em hard. Knock em out.

JAIL

A: How are the cops around here?

AS: Terrible. I don't know how it go because every time I see them and they see me, I run.

S: Why?

AS: They're the bad guys. They put you in they car and they take you to places you don't want to go. For nothing.

S: You been in jail before?

AS: Yeah. The first time I stole a car I was like twelve.

A: How'd you get caught?

AS: Oh man, my stupid self, look, riding around by my school—bang—I see a little female. I'm like yeah. She get in the car. All I know, I look in the rear mirror, I see the police behind me. So they hit the siren. All I know, I started jamming it. I'm gone! I'm flat. My stupid ass went up a one-way right up there by a police station. All I know they must of told other people—beaucoup police cars comin. So I'm booking back down Alvar and I ran into a pole by the stoplight. I tried to run and the man tackled me.

A: What happened to the female?

AS: I don't know what happened to her. I worry about me! She ain't hurt, but I haven't talked to her since then.

A: Kind of blew your chances with her, huh?

AS: I don't know, probably. Probably get something in my name, probably pick her up.

S: What happened when you went to jail?

AS: In jail? All types of stuff! They didn't want to feed me.

S: You were scared in there?

AS: I wasn't scared. I wanted my mama, though. But I was in there about twelve, a long time ago. Like three years ago.

S: Is that the only time you've gone?

AS: Uh huh. Uh huh.

S: Ooh! What else you did?

AS: The last time, [it] happened [was] with a man in the French Quarters. I was just bored that day and whacked a man. The police hacked me up but I got out the same night.

A: For what?

AS: Nothin, I was bored. That's a tradition in the French Quarters around Mardi Gras season.

A: How did you get caught?

AS: Laughin, after I did it. And I didn't know the man was a policeman—he was undercover and he arrested me.

A: You whacked an undercover man?

AS: Well, his friend was the undercover man. The man I whacked. That was his friend.

S: Whaaa?

AV: Yeah. But I got out the next day.

34

A: Did you get prosecuted?

AS: Uh huh, I don't know why they never sent the court pages, the man mustn't have wanted to press charges. Then I went to jail for another stolen car. I was like thirteen. But I didn't know it was stolen. Well, I knew it was stolen, but I didn't know it was *stolen* stolen.

S: What you mean?

AS: All right, I knew the car was stolen but I didn't know it was *stolen* stolen. I thought somebody jacked somebody from waaaay out of town and they just switched the license plate, so I got that charge. I stole the car from a dude that stole the car.

I got caught with that. But, that wasn't no high-speed chase or nothing. The police saw me goin into the car with a big old flat head. I didn't try to run, I was tired. I try to talk my way out of it saying I was trying to fix the car. He put me in the car, curse me out. I went to jail for that. Came home like three days later.

Yeah, then I went to jail—all us went to jail. Me, Heavy D, Ronald, Derrick, yeah—that was this summer. Riding in a car, right down Gallier, it's about four something in the morning, and D didn't even have on his lights. The police pulled us over— they found crack, weed—I don't know where it came from. I don't know who that was for but all of us went to jail fast. I just beat that charge. Not guilty! They say the police wrote the papers wrong.

And after that I went to jail for slapping a girl on the shoulder. Like people be walking by and we slap em on the shoulder and look the other way, make em think somebody else did it. Well, we be doing that with like a crowd of us and the police saw me. And I went to jail and came out the same day. Simple battery and harassment. I'm still fighting that charge.

S: Do you consider yourself violent?

AS: Not really. I'm not the kind of violent person you don't want to be around or you scared to be around. I ain't like that.

S: You just occasionally sneak somebody?

AS: Uh huh.

MOVING

S: What y'all move for?

AS: Oh, well, my mama didn't like the house. Well, she didn't like the environment. We cool, but she likes for me to really hang inside.

S: But you don't want to be inside?

AS: Shit, I'll be inside if I have some good company. It's different. Like outside you can be like, "fuck-you." Something like that. To people inside you got to be like, "Man, you can't really be like." See outside you're freer. Inside you just got to remain calm and chill. Yeah.

S: Rules.

AS: I can whack people outside. I can't whack nobody inside. It's boring. See if I had a game, I'd probably stay inside a little more.

A: If you had a game?

AS: A Playstation 2. I got the money, but I ain't never go get one, though.

A: Is New Orleans a good city to live in?

AS: I can't say. I never went out of New Orleans, except for Mississippi.

S: If you had the choice of livin in another neighborhood, I'm guessin you wouldn't go, but would you?

AS: Yeah!

S: I thought you liked it around here.

AS: I like it around here, but I want to move to the East. Where all the females are, you understand.

S: Do you think you'd be a better person if you lived somewhere else?

AS: Probably. To be honest, probably.

S: Why you say?

AS: Different environment. You know—how shall I put this? Let me see. I can move into another environment but I'm just chillin, you know. I can adapt to another environment, yeah I like that.

S: So you could live in a predominantly white environment?

AS: Yeah.

S: And be tight with everyone around there?

AS: Oh no!

S: Why?

AS: No, I'm just saying, cuz you know that's my friend, but I wouldn't get in no trouble or nothing around there; I just be chillin. I can live around there, but I still be around here.

[sirens]

A: How come you'd be cool livin around white people but you'd never be tight?

AS: If they seem cool, I'll be cool with em—

A: But they could never be your people?

AS: Yeah, they could be my people. I don't discriminate nobody. They wouldn't be as close as my people round here. I ain't grow up with em. I never smoke no weed with them.

DIPSET

A: Any parting words, any other stories you want to tell us?

AS: Uh huh. Dipset.

A: What's that mean?

AS: It's official. That means like, "We're about to go." Or if you're telling a female "dipset" that mean pop me off. But dipset—it means like leavin, or going somewhere, or how you rockin. And early—that just makes the sentence fire like—"The block pumpin early"—see what I'm saying? You see how fire that sound? See, like me, I like to come with new slang for the streets. The hot peeps that I am, you understand, I got to give them hot speak make them feel like hot people like me. So that's basically it.

ARLET: MARIO

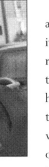

A lot of the time I sit on the balcony just to think and clear my mind. Once Mario starts talking to me it puts me in a better mood. He's tall, gaunt, and has really big feet. His voice travels a long distance. He tries to make himself seem conceited by pretending he's a superstar. He'll say things like, "No pictures today. No pictures. Thank you." He dresses really well. I don't know where or how he gets clothes big or long enough to fit him. And every time he hears a beat he starts doing some kind of dance.

Whenever you see him on the Ave. He's always happy. Maybe it's because he feels like he's at home. One thing I admire about him is no matter what anyone says about him, he's still confident with himself. He makes whatever people say into a joke. In response to people talking about his feet all the time, he now calls himself Ninth Ward Foots.

SAM: NINTH WARD FOOTS

I was outside again, as usual, smoking my cigarette and watching cars go by, hoping I see Roulette get off the bus. A few minutes earlier, she called and said she was on her way.

It was kind of dark. Not completely, like how it is late at night, but dark enough to have your preteen kids inside. There weren't too many people outside, just pedestrians and Mario.

While I was in the process of smoking my cigarette, I saw like three police cars stop on my block. The police around here are very picky. They don't just check anybody; they check people who blend in with the environment. And you can easily tell who blends in by their level of comfort. I guess they saw that Mario was pretty comfortable and decided to harass him for no reason. Well, no good reason anyway. They saw these other people walk right past and they didn't even look at them. They went straight for Mario. To be honest, my guess is that they were racist. The people walking past were all white people and so was the police.

While they were approaching him, I started taking a longer and a harder puffs at my cigarette. My nerves started to get aggravated and I was trying to soothe them, but all I could think in my head was, "Awww, that's messed up."

They told him to get on his knees, hollering like he had committed a crime, "Get down, get down now and put your hands on your head!" Mario was looking confused, like "What did I do?" while slowly following their orders. They then made him lay on the ground and started checking him for anything illegal. It seemed like they just wanted a reason to take him in.

After they searched him and found nothing, they told him to get up. After he did they got in their car and left. Mario didn't say a word. He just looked confused and walked home.

PICK-UPS

I.

Saturday evening almost seven o'clock Lemon, B, Mario, Butter, and Derick all sit on our porch complimenting some girl who just passed. Not giving anyone else a chance, Mario automatically tries to say hello at her. He gets rejected. I feel kinda bad for him, I know he feels played too because when the girl doesn't stop to talk to him he start ribbin her and calling her everything but the child of God. I'm waiting to see if this is going to lead to a big confrontation but it doesn't. The girl walks off as if he's beneath her and answering him would put her at his level. While B, Lemon, Butter, and Derick all buck Mario's head up to curse the girl out even more, and point out her flaws so they would laugh. —Arlet

II.

It was 8:30 pm. I was sitting on the balcony when some slim boy with a bush fade started running real fast onto the neutral ground and across the street.

He ran onto somebody's porch and jumped over the gate. He was running from the police. About three seconds later a policeman jumped over the gate with a flashlight in his hand. Two minutes later the policeman hopped over the fence and got back in his car and drove away. It all happened so quickly. The policeman seemed to be pissed off, but I thought the situation was rather funny. —Sam

III.

Sitting on the porch as usual, bored, listening to a few boys talking about punks. A boy named Twine talks about a punk stalking him in the club. I'm wondering, "Why you still be going to this club if someone's stalking you?" Another boy sits back and listens for a while and then mouths off about what he'd do, "If he ever play with me, Imma knock dat boy out."

Twine quickly objects, "Boy, no you not. That boy be too deep. I guarantee you, nothing but G-Nikes and Timberlands gonna be in your face once you start swinging." Now I'm wondering, "What kind of punk has that much power?" Twine says, "That's why all I tell him is, 'I don't rock like that,' if he try to come at me." —Arlet

LEMON

These days, Lemon is always joking around with somebody or making fun of the people he chills with for kicks. From what I see, he especially likes to aggravate Arlet. Strangely, he's a little more loose since he got shot.

Now, don't get me wrong. He's not all goofy all the time. He usually has his serious moments, too. Just let somebody try to get over on him and watch how serious he gets. One thing he doesn't play around with is money—his image tells that by how he dresses.

Lemon is cool to chill around. You can easily keep a steady conversation with him—just don't make him mad. He doesn't tolerate bullshit from anybody. And to be honest, I think he's a little too much heart and boldness for his own good. I mean, the dude got shot and still hangs around the same spot, betting someone won't do it again.—Sam

I went on the porch just to see who was outside. I see Lemon and he says, "Wuz up?" and I respond, "Nothing."

Taking a seat in the doorway I can see him dancing to the beat of a song playing in a passing car, "Drop and give me fifty," by Tenth Ward Buck. I laugh because as hard as he seems to be, he likes to dance and actually knows how. I can see Twine, B, Snake and Lemon's cousin bucking him up. They start talking about going to the club. Lemon says, "That bitch be hanging in the club, I'm telling you. For real."

I've known Lemon for almost ten years. I've never known his real name. We used to play with him all the time saying his real name was Le'Mon, a French name. But, for a long time, I never had a real conversation with him because we weren't allowed to talk to the boys who hung in front of our house.

As years went by, he became friends with Ariel and I got to be better acquainted with him. When he would see me on the balcony, he'd speak to me and ask where my sister was. But then, he hardly ever told me to call her. I guess he just wanted to make conversation. Their relationship stayed on a friendly level—no physical attraction.

A couple of years later he went to jail. It must have been a serious crime because he was gone for at least four years. When he came back, I had grown up and he became interested in me. He claimed he could take care of me and could buy me this, that, and the other. Most of the promises he made went through one ear and came out the other. There were days he tried to play the whole sincere role like he really meant business. I admired him because he didn't give up; he never stopped talking or speaking to me like some of the boys around my house did. He just brushed it off and tried again.

One day, it was real cold outside, but I was sitting out on the porch because I had just finished arguing with my dad. I still had tears in my eyes from crying. I had a pair of shorts and a t-shirt on. I didn't care that I was under-dressed because I just wanted

to get out of the house. After maybe five minutes, Lemon walked out of the store. He looked up and saw me. This time, he didn't talk to me about being his girlfriend, and he made me feel better. He saw how I was dressed and gave me his sweater. That was so sweet of him—from then on I took some of the things he said to be kind of true, instead of not believing anything. —Arlet

ARLET: TWINE

Remembering people on my block is kinda hard because a lot of people have come and gone. They might live in another neighborhood or stop hanging in my neighborhood or just pass every now and again. But one person I distinctively remember and have known ever since I was eleven years old is this boy named Twine. My sister Ariel had a big crush on him. He was always dressed nice; hair was always kept up—he was just a neat person. Eventually, he became appealing to both of us. He was a new face on our block and cute at the same time. Our fascination grew.

When he came around I would get excited just as much as Ariel. If I was in the back room, she would call me and say, "Twine outside," and I'd say "Girl, for real?" and we'd both take off running to the living room window. When we went to the stairs, he was always there and Ariel and I talked to him about nothing. She stayed downstairs longer than me and eventually the conversation stopped being the three of us to just the two of them. Ariel used to go downstairs and chill with him or walk around the corner to be away from everyone and everything. Their long conversations ended and now they just speak whenever they see each other.

I always said he was the coolest boy that hung downstairs in front of my house. He wasn't like some of the boys who made girls look bad calling out their names or saying how nasty they are. He was quiet for the most part, and it seemed like he kept to himself. That's what I like most about him—he had respect for girls and wasn't about telling his business to the Ave. boys. He always told me they talked too much, and that's how people get a reputation.

His clothes aren't three sizes bigger than his body, he doesn't look hard, like he's had a hard life or doesn't care about nothing or nobody. Maybe that's why the police never bothered him as much as they do the average black teenage boy hanging on the streets.

Days when I was sitting on the porch, he would speak to me before he went into the store. He always asked me about school and whether I had a boyfriend. I knew he didn't like me—I was too young and he liked my sister. He probably asked me because people used to say I was mean, and that made him curious. Eventually, I became closer to him and I got to know him a lot better.

When he did get arrested outside of my house a few years later, something felt empty on the Avenue. His face wasn't there, his smile was gone, and our conversation with him was lost.

While he was in jail then for awhile after, Twine stopped hanging on the block all together. When he came back, we were closer than ever—more than anyone would know. I got so comfortable with him, I talked to him about my problems and he would give me advice—always positive. There were some nights when I'd go downstairs and talk about him to just check up on his life. One thing Twine did whenever he saw me, he greeted me with a hug. Some of those days he did it, it was exactly what I needed.

Twine used to always tell me, "Man it's hard out here," and I began to wonder why is it so hard. There have been numerous occasions when he has told me that having a legit job is not enough to make ends meet and that's why he has another job on the side. Speaking things into existence is what he does a lot. If he says that he's addicted to the streets, he won't be able to leave them. But Twine is the type of person who can do whatever he puts his mind to. If he wants it, he has the potential and ability to be whatever he wants in life.

ARLET: INTERVIEW WITH TWINE

Arlet: I'm here with Twine and we're here on the block. Why did you choose to do an interview?

Twine: Only on the strength on you. You told me you needed to do an interview, and if I can help you out, I'll do it.

A: How do you feel about me interviewing you?

T: I feel comfortable. I feel cool with it. It's all good.

A: If you could describe yourself in one word what would it be?

T: Real.

A: Why did you move here?

T: My mama moved here. Talk to my mama cuz I didn't really move here, ya dig? I was livin with my moms.

A: How old were you when you moved here?

T: Probably like seven.

A: And before living around here, where did you live?

T: In the Desire [Public Housing Development].

A: How many brothers and sisters do you have?

T: I have five brothers and one sister.

A: Are you and your family close?

T: Yeah, we're real close: brothers, mama. My daddy dead. I'm not close to that man—he wasn't part of the family anyway. But we dealt with him. Ain't no beef, ain't nothin.

A: What makes you close?

T: Just love. It's that love we got for each other in our house. Moms is the top of the family tree, so as long as moms together we're together.

A: Who is one person you look up to and admire?

T: My mama. She's a strong black woman; a person who's done it by herself. I respect her for that—she didn't have nobody. My grandma was there, but she passed—God bless her soul. I really look up to my mom. She made a way for us and she took care of us. And I'm happy. I got one of those moms that's focused, not out on the street on drugs. A hard workin lady. I respect her to the fullest. Yeah, she the one. Still is.

A: What are your hobbies?

T: I work out, I go to the gym, play basketball, play football—that's what I do. Read a book sometimes to ease my mind when I get off from work. That's how I get by. Go and chill on the block with the fellas.

SCHOOL

A: Did you graduate high school?

T: Yes. Yes. Yes.

A: And how old are you?

T: I'm twenty.

A: And why you not in college?

T: [pause] I had a little problem. I was supposed to go, but something happened. Something terrible happened, you know what I'm saying, shattered my little hopes. So, I still could go. I got a good opportunity of going, you know what I'm saying? I ain't stopping. I'm still trying to get there, ya dig, but it's just a slow process, you understand, got to have patience. But I'm gonna get there.

A: How important is school to you?

T: It's real important. You need that for living. There's nothing like knowledge, living right. I wouldn't be out here if I had the knowledge, if I was in school: a good life, hope, balance in your life.

THE STREETS

A: What you mean "out here."

T: In the streets. That's what I mean.

A: Why are you in the streets? I mean, you have a house, right?

T: Yeah, I got a house. It's hard. Something attract me to the streets. When you're hungry, ya dig and your stomach go to hurting and moms can't do it, moms workin a 9 to 5, I'm tired of seeing mom struggle so I had to get out there and get her.

A: What do you do for money?

T: I work hard. I'm a hard working young man, ya dig, do a little carpentry work on the sides. I get down like that, that's how I get my money, you know.

A: Ninety-five percent of the time you're outside on this block, why is that?

T: I just like to hang. Chill. Relax. You know, the block move me, you know what I'm saying? When I came on the block it just move me. I just fell in love with it, so I'm stuck with it, you know.

A: How are you like the boys that hang on this block and how are you different?

T: I don't know how I'm like em. I'm my own man. I'm different from the flock. The only thing we got in common is we hang on the block. Even though I have those evil ways, you know, I feel I'm different. I got the good side in me. This rest of em, they're all out.

A: What types of things do you discuss on this block?

T: All types of things. Life. Money. How to get this money. How we gonna make it. Where we're gonna be in the next twenty years. We talk to each other like men. We is men. Life. Family. Marriage. We talk some crazy shit, but we talk some good stuff, too. We discuss everything on the block.

A: Okay. Um, if you could change one thing about your block, what would it be?

T: The police.

A: Whatchu mean?

T: The aggravating ass police.

A: That's the only thing that you would change?

T: Ain't nothing else that need to be changed on this block—it's just all love.

A: Do they sell drugs on this block?

Pause.

T: They do a little something, you understand. They do a little something—they got their slingin, you know what I'm saying? They bang.

A: You don't think they need to change that?

T: Hey, that's life, you know what I'm saying.

A: How is that life?

T: That's been going on since before we was out here. You know what I'm saying?

A: But it's makin it worse.

T: Hey, they made it worse on us, you know what I'm saying?

A: How could you want to change the police being around here, if they doing stuff that's illegal?

T: They've got some brothers out here that are workin their ass off, you know what I'm saying, and they still ain't getting no work down there. You got to get it how you live, you know what I'm saying? At first I was like, that shit wasn't power. But hey, shit, you gotta live, you gotta eat, you gotta feed, and down here, shhh, you wear your ass out, you got to work three jobs to get out of here.

VIOLENCE

A: If you had a choice to live in another neighborhood, would you?

T: I do live in another neighborhood. I moved, but you know, I still come back in the hood, like an addiction, you know what I'm saying. I don't know. I don't know.

A: How could make your block better?

T: More money. Simplest plan: more money.

A: What would you do with the money?

T: I would put it in the houses and shit around here, make sure the people don't starve or nothing because they do got some starving people out here, you know what I'm saying and I'm one of em—so, that's how I'd better the block, you know what I'm saying, make sure all my people feed. Eat, you know what I'm saying.

A: Do you think your block can change?

T: Yeah, it could change. Ain't nothing wrong with the block to me, but it could change for the better. I feel like it's right like this.

A: Have there been any killings on this block?

T: They've had many killings on this block. Plenty. Seen them with my own eyes. Yeah, they had plenty.

A: Would you say there are a lot of people out here that do drugs? On drugs.

T: They got a bunch of em that are on drugs, you know what I'm saying. Marijuana is a drug, huh? So, they got a bunch of em on it. Not everybody, you know what I'm saying, but the majority. You understand, the majority. The majority get high, trying to get by.

A: What is the worst thing about your block?

T: Just the hate. Just the shit they do out here. They hate like crazy around here. The hate and the greed.

A: Why? Because one is making more than the other?

T: That's what it is, yeah. That's what it is.

A: Do you get along with everyone on your block?

T: I get along with everybody. Everybody cool with me. I'm cool with everybody, you know. It's all good with me—I get along with everybody. The old lady across the street—everybody!

A: Do you think you would be a better person if you lived somewhere else?

T: I don't know. I can't say, you know what I'm saying. I probably would have been the same or worser. I can't say, I don't know, you know. I don't know, I really can't tell you that, you dig. It's all good how I am now, you know, how I'm doin now, how I'm rockin, so – hey.

A: Do you fear anything about this block?
T: No, not really. I grew to love it. I don't see no fear in it. It ain't like no scary place to me.

A: Do you consider yourself a violent person?

T: No, not at all. A sweet kind man, you know, but

at the same time, I'll roll with it. I ain't no violent man. The truth—I'm real, but I ain't no violent person. Nah. Mmm. Mm.

A: Have you ever been arrested on this block?

T: Yeah, I've been arrested on this block. About three times.

A: How old were you the first time?

T: I think I was bout fourteen, fifteen. About fifteen. Then I went back when I was seventeen, and then I bounced back when I was like twenty, ya dig. So it was three times I went.

A: The first time you went to jail, what you went to jail for?

T: Possession for marijuana.

A: How long did you stay in there?

T: I didn't stay in there that long. Probably like a good month.

A: What was it like?

T: Shit. Crap. What was it like? It was terrible in that motherfucker. I don't want to go in there anymore. It's bad. They handle you bad in there—terrible. Worse fucking day of my life—jail, the worse day of my life. I don't want to go in there. It's ter-

rible in there. I regret it. I swear to God.

A: Where do you see yourself in the next four or five years?

T: Shit, I don't know. That's sad when I don't know. I want to do a lot. I don't know where life is going to take me, if I'm going to be livin or not. I want to be a club owner. There are so many things that I want. I want to get into the real estate business. I want to be a carpenter. I got plenty of things. But I don't know how life is going to]take its toll on me. I can't really say. I can't predict the future

ARLET: KIM

When I told Kim I was writing about her, she smiled and said, "You can write anything you want about me. You can talk about my problem, anything." I was so excited that she agreed to do it. I first met Kim when I was a little girl. She was always tall and skinny. I knew her because of her usual sales. She sold shoes, shirts, hats—anything she could to make money, and my mom bought something every time.

I tried to schedule an interview with her, but I couldn't catch up with her so I talked to my mom instead.

Arlet: How did you first meet Kim?

Emelda: I met her probably selling something, cuz she does that a lot to get money.

A: What kinds of things does she sell?

E: She would sell mostly clothes or household items—anything she thought she could get money for. Sometimes she'll want money for food. Or sometimes she would just be blunt and say, "Well, you know what I do. And I just need to get me something. I need to get high." Or, "I need to get me a hit," or something like that. And being a female and understanding where she was coming from, [I bought] a lot of the stuff I probably didn't need or didn't want. I would rather give her the money than for her to prostitute herself, basically, for money.

A: What kind of person did Kim appear to be to you?

E: At first, when I met her, she just seemed like the

typical female that smokes rock. Always hype. Always selling something. Walking up and down the avenue. She seemed to be a person that was very humorous. When I first met her, mostly what I liked about Kim was that she was honest. Sometimes she wouldn't have anything to sell, she would just say— she calls me moms, momma or by my nickname Button: "I just wanna get something to eat. Could you help me out? Could you give me a dollar? Fifty cents, a quarter?" And she'd say, "I'll pay you back on such and such a day." And most of the time, she would. And that's what I admired about her. If Kim didn't have the money, she would just give me something.

One Mother's Day, I was having a bad evening when I came home from my mother-in-law's house. When we pulled up that night, she asked me how my day was, told me happy Mother's Day and stuff. I told her it wasn't good. And she just reached out her hand, and took my hand, and she just put something in my hand, and said, "Well, I hope this makes your day better." And she just kept walking. In her little fast, usual way, [she] kept going on about her business.

I don't know if I opened my hand right then and there downstairs, or if I waited until I got inside, but when

I opened my hand, it was five dollars. And that was something that I never forgot about Kim because I never had a person in her predicament just to walk up and give me anything. Most people like that, their mentality is to take. Or to get over. Because they're sick. But even with her habit, she wasn't that type of person. It was simple, it wasn't a lot, but it came from the heart, and she meant it. And ever since that day, we just had a real good relationship. She would always ask about the children; she would always talk to the children in a positive way. She would be very open and honest about her situation.

I know sometimes she gets off track. At one point, I don't know what she did, but we didn't see her for a long time. She went to jail. When she came back, she had gained a lot of weight and had sent her children off to another state because she wanted a better life for her children.

Still with all of that, sometimes she'll try to lie to me. Like one day it was cold, and she was trying to sell me a jacket [that] still had the price tag on it.

And I said, "Kim, I'm not gonna take your jacket cuz it's cold." She said, "Oh, well, I got another one at home. Just give me five or six dollars." I was about to give her the money but she turned back and said, "No, no, no – I don't want it. I'm not gonna take your money cuz I'm lying." And she said, "I know you gonna worry about me if you know that I didn't have a jacket." And I admired that. She recognizes people that care about her. When I see her, even if it's been a long time, we will just walk up to each other and embrace each other and, she might embrace the children.

A: Do you ever remember Kim when she was sober?

E: Yeah, I've seen her sober. It was after she had gotten out of jail and she had gained a lot of weight. When she wasn't on drugs for that period of time, her whole way of dress was different. Everything was always together. Her hair was fixed. Her clothes were neat. She had her children in private school and it was a good school cuz my children went to the same school. And she would participate and go to pick up their report cards, and go to conferences. And it was like being a real mom. You know, things that a normal mom would do.

A: Did Kim ever have a permanent house, or did she live on the street?

E: No, she's always had somewhere to go. She lives with her mom. I would imagine her mom doesn't like what she does, because she's tried to get her to move away to another state. At one point, her mom left when she was in jail. And when she came back, she moved away for a little time with her mom. But then the whole family came back to New Orleans.

SAM: TATTOOS AND WOUNDS

Just about everyone around my house has either a tattoo or a wound, and most have both. Most tell what type of life you live, others are just for decoration, but all have a story behind them.

Mario has tattoos of the words Ave. Boy Foots. This means he's always on the avenue of St. Claude, and he has big feet.

Lemon has a couple gun shot wounds. They represent how he lives on the edge. He takes his chances and seems to not care what the results are. He won't change his lifestyle.

Other people have tattoos saying Ninth Ward, meaning that's where they usually are or where they were born, and that's cool, representing where you live but it's also dangerous.

I have two tattoos myself. Mine are the names of the two people I really care about. These are the names of my son and my future wife. I've decided to get these names because these people, besides my family, are my reason to life.

I'll never forget the week that I got the tattoo for Roulette. It was the beginning of summer and I went away for a four day sheetrock job in Alabama with my dad and brother Malcolm. The four days stretched into two weeks, and every night with my muscles

aching, I called Roulette. The whole time I was away she stayed in my room.

The money was good, and all of my expenses were taken care of, so I went and got a tattoo—RUDY—on my shoulder. It made me feel good to think about having her on my shoulder. While I was putting up sheetrock during the day, I would run my fingers over the place where the tattoo was scabbing up and smile at how it would make her happy to see it there.

The night we were coming home, I called her and told her we were on the way. We got in at four in the morning and everyone was asleep except Roulette. She had stayed awake the whole night waiting on me to get home.

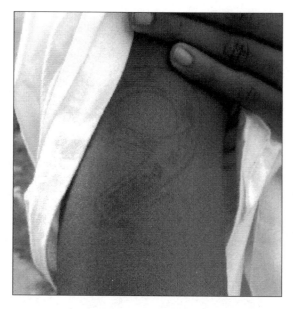

She hugged me hard, and wouldn't let me go. Eventually I pulled myself away, and went to clean up. While I was washing all the sheetrock mud out of my hair and ears, she cooked. After I ate, she massaged my sore muscles. We drifted off to sleep as the sun was coming up, and she patted my back, calming me and singing the song she wrote for me, "I love my baby Sammy."

Getting a tattoo your first time is so scary, especially after watching someone else get one first. The noise of the needle is stuck in your head, taunting you like the thoughts before getting a shot. At least when you're getting a shot, it's over in a few seconds.

When you're getting a tattoo, it's everything you expected it to be. It hurts. It hurts the whole time you're getting it and after it's done. Just envision a sharp needle, slightly larger than the needles you see at the doctor, stabbing you fifteen times per second. Keep in mind that the person drawing your tattoo has to take their time and go slow so that they don't mess up. After they finish, they usually go over it a second time, and that burns like a lit match.

ARLET: INTERVIEW WITH GWEN

Ms. Gwen Lee is a lady on my block who runs a beauty salon. When I was growing up, she came off as bossy. It seemed like she was always telling someone what to do. But everyone that talks about her has great things to say, so I wanted to get to know her. One day, I saw her outside of her shop selling DVDs and CDs. She invited me to her church and I asked her for this interview. I found out a lot more than I expected.

Arlet: Where were you raised?

Gwn: In the Seventh Ward. There used to be the barroom Heaven's Gate. That used to be our house. It was an upstairs and downstairs house. It burned down in 1975.

A: Okay. Why did you want to open up a beauty shop?

G: I've been doing hair for thirty years. I'm a licensed barber, cosmetologist and manicurist; and [I'm an] instructor of each. I've had a shop since 1987, and I taught at Moler Beauty College. I just stopped teaching two years ago because I took ill.

A: How long have you been in business on this block?

G: I bought the building in 1995 and I opened up in '96.

A: What made you want to open up a shop here?

G: I've lived in the Ninth Ward thirty years, and I was looking [to move from the Seventh Ward to] something where they had a lot of traffic, and it was the ideal spot. One night, I was on my way home from work, and I was passing this building. I saw it had "For Sale—L. Austin" on it. I pulled in front of the building and I said, "Where do I know that name from? I know L. Austin."

I couldn't picture who L. Austin was. I went home and I told my husband. He said, "Why you don't know the name? That's your pastor name!" It didn't dawn on me. He's my assistant pastor. I got him on the telephone, and I told him. He said, "Ms. Lee, you don't wanna buy that building." And I said, "Yes I do." It was sitting empty.

A: This used to be a daycare.

G: Mmhmm. I left it empty and I didn't do anything with it for a year until my sister and them kept on saying, 'What did you get it for?" I said, "I got it because I was gonna open the shop, but I'm trying to figure out how I'm gonna do it. I don't know if I can make the easy move with my clients from here to there." And all of the sudden, I did it. I didn't have any money after I bought the building; I was broke cuz I paid cash in cash without any financing. That was money I saved—I worked two jobs. And I saved it. When they told me how much it was, I had it. I bought it straight out like that. And then after that, I had maybe $125 left in the bank. I didn't have enough money to buy chairs or anything.

John Jay had a warehouse in Slidell where the school was. And I called them and I asked, "Do you have any chairs and stuff?" I said, "Do you know who I am?"

"Yeah, you work for Moler." He said, "If you get a truck, come to Slidell." My husband was out of town, so I called a friend named Jimmy [and] he brought a truck. We went to Slidell. See these chairs right here? He gave me every last one of these chairs for ten dollars. Then these [other] chairs were sixty dollars each. Every week I went down and paid him. Every week. He put it on a layaway plan for me.

Whatever anybody loaned me, I paid them back double. Everybody. I didn't have a problem getting nothing from nobody. I just went one day at a time. Then I had good people that worked for me at the time. My shop had fourteen people in it. They said, "Whatever you don't have, we're not worried about it." You know, it's been a struggle—don't get me wrong, but it's a good struggle. It's by faith.

A: Why did you pick the name Secrets?

G: When I was working for Moler Beauty College— and this is the truth—I was under contract and we couldn't have a beauty salon. I opened a salon anyway, and I just called it Secrets, because it was my secret. [Most of the people who work here] I had in beauty school. In barber school.

A: Everybody who's working here.

G: Uh huh. I had them in school. I'm very seldom here. They each have a key of their own, and they take good care of it. They call me if they have a real serious problem. But I've been doing that for five years – I haven't really been here. I can't stay for too long because of the chemicals.

BUSINESS ON ST. CLAUDE

A: Would you consider living here?

G: I do. I live in the Ninth Ward on Congress Street!

A: Is this about the same or different than where you were raised?

G: Yes, a lot. I was raised years ago, so the drugs weren't as prominent as they are now. And if they was, I didn't know anything about it, because I was too young. And then it was hidden from me. Now I'm grown, so I can see what flourishes in front of me.

A: All right. What do you like about this block?

G: The clients. The way the neighborhood is structured—multicultured.

A: What would you change about this block?

G: The drugs. That's basically the only thing that I would change is the flow of drugs that's active in the neighborhood. It brings the wrong kind of people into the neighborhood: people that's looking for drugs. And I think that the police don't have a real handle on the drug situation in the Ninth Ward—not in the Bywater area.

A: What is your relationship with the people that hang on this block?

G: I have a very good relationship with the people in the block, because I talk to everybody. I try to communicate [with] each person on their own level, and not be above anybody, because I'm not.

I get a lot of respect. Everybody around here is like, "Okay, there's Ms. Gwen. Oh, Ms. Gwen's outside! I don't have a problem with anybody in the neighborhood. I like to give a little barbeque now and then, and give a little something to everybody. Every holiday I have gifts for whoever comes in. But that's just life. You know, if somebody die, I always raise money and bring it to the mom or whoever.

There are situations that happen in this neighborhood, like killings and you can go and ask some of the people would they like to donate something, or would they like to give something? They don't. The businesses won't give, and the reason why they won't give, because they feel like it's not their problem, when it actually is their problem, because it's a neighborhood thing. I see the same people at the funerals. If I go to a funeral, your mom and them is there. It's the same people. Cuz everybody around here know each other, so everybody should really go.

A: What's so good about owning a business on this block?

G: Well, the flow of traffic is good, because we get the notoriety that we need. But the people in the neighborhood support our business more than outsiders.

A: Have you ever thought about relocating?

G: No I haven't. I've thought about opening another Secrets, but I wouldn't call it Secrets, I would call it something else. I wouldn't want nobody to know it was me.

Abram: It would be Secret's Secrets.

G: No, it would be Hidden Places.

ARLET'S GENERATION

Abram: You have children?

G: Two. One lives in Oklahoma and one lives in Tacoma, Washington. They're both in the service. They're stateside. None of them have been on foreign land.

Abram: Tell us a story about St. Claude that we don't know.

G: I like St. Claude Avenue. I mean, it's quiet in the morning, it's loud all during the day when it should be quiet [when] people should be in school. And in the evening time, everybody's out and about. It's like Canal Street used to be, except that we don't have the department stores.

Abram: What do you think about John Mac?

G: I think they need to get a handle on it. If the kids don't want to go to school, in my opinion, they don't go. Wear your hair proper. Pull the pants up. Put the belts on. What's the pants down for? That's jailhouse mentality, to me. You don't want nothing as far as I'm concerned.

[One time] I gave [my son] seventy-five dollars; he was supposed to go get a pair of pants and a shirt for a dance. When he came to Moler's School of Beauty, I said, "Let me see your pants?" They were too big. I said, "Give me my receipt, and give me the clothes." He said, "Oh mommy, if I wear this, I'm gonna be a nerd." I say, "Well, guess what son? You're gonna be a nerd. Cuz you're not going out here with those pants falling down on you like that." He refused to go to the dance! But tell me now, today, at thirty, don't he thank me?

Abram: I was interested in how Ms. Gwen sees you, Arlet.

G: How I see her? I could tell you! I see her as a very respectable young lady. She don't carry herself like a lot of them do around here. She don't disrespect herself. I don't think she's allowed to. It's the way you're raised.

A: What do you mean as far as disrespecting yourself?

G: As far as standing outside, cursing, hooping and hollering: M-F this, and M-F that. I don't hear you saying that. And don't think I don't see you, because I do. (Laughs) But I know you're not allowed – your brother either! None of y'all. Y'all not allowed to just rip and run. People see that. You're raised in a dif-

ferent way. And that's good. That's real good. You look like you wanna get somewhere in life. That's how I see her. Like she gonna be somebody – maybe President or something.

And Guess what? You don't need name brand clothes. You could go to Wal-Mart. People don't believe that!

A: Oh, I know. I'm glad I wasn't raised like that—to have all that high fashion and-

G: You don't have to have someone else name on you. It could be your name!

A: That's what I said!

G: If you got to have name brands, go to the thrift store and buy em. That's what I do. I still do that. It's what you save that's gonna help you in the long run, not what you making. You got to learn to put it away for a rainy day. And something that you really, really want! It'll come to you when you realize what it is. Believe me.

ARLET: THIS WHOLE DRUG THING

Drugs are a really big issue on my block. Most people think it's just another way of life, another job, or just another thing to do. It's taken lightly by people of all ages, but I think it makes or breaks you. When you begin selling drugs, it helps you make fast money and you can keep up with the latest fashions and buy other material things. Most of the drug selling is for more of your wants than needs. A lot of people say they sell drugs until they get enough money to get away, move out of town, or help their family, but how do you know when it's enough? They just get caught up.

I didn't think of any drug as a moral problem, I thought of it as being addictive, because I see the effect it has on people I'm close to or see around. Marijuana was always a turn off in boys because a person close to me used to smoke and then went to a higher drug which eventually led to heroin. Now his whole appearance has changed.

Growing up in my household, cigarettes were smoked when the feeling of depression weighed in. I hated them but my mother liked them well enough to smoke them every now and again. She'll smoke them on the porch when something happened to one of us, or when she would fuss with my dad. For years, smoking wasn't a habit, but now it is because my mom is more stressed than ever. I know because she takes medication, her hair is shedding, and she's not eating. If she doesn't have cigarettes in her truck and we're too far from home, she'll go to the store and buy a whole other pack. I can't say too much of anything because she works and can spend her money on whatever she wants to spend it on. It gets worse, because Sam and Martin are smoking now, too. Now half of my mother's children are into the habit of smoking. Riding in the car in the morning, three cigarettes are lit and it feels like they're all trying to blow the smoke in my face.

Sam sometimes drinks because of some of the problems he's having with girls and his son. I feel a lot of them could have been prevented if he would have listened to my mother and the advice she gives him.

Sam's problems bother me a lot. He often separates himself from the rest of us and that's not healthy. He's torturing himself by trying to fight off his problems by smoking and drinking. Sometimes I feel he needs to let his problems and give them to God. When he drinks he scares me because he does and says anything and often starts arguments that don't need to happen. Sometimes I feel he will hurt someone or someone is going to hurt him. All he has to do is sit, talk, and laugh with his family and I guarantee that would make him feel a hundred times better.

SAM: MONDAYS

It's Monday and as usual it's empty outside. The store under my house is closed. It seems as though whenever the downstairs store is closed cars don't even pass by. Even the barbershop on the corner of Piety is closed, so it's even quieter.

I like days like this. The only problem is that whenever I want a snack, I have to walk a half block down to the corner store. But I guess that's a good trade—a day of peace and quiet in exchange for a short walk. The temperature is just right. Not quite cool enough for a sweater, but enough to where you need to wear two shirts. It kind of makes you want to just sit outside with a beer, a telephone, and a pack of Kools, and just enjoy the rest of the day.

PART III: LOOKING BACK INSIDE

A lot of times, people in my neighborhood think that our family is more than it really is. They think we have perfect relationships and don't have money problems since we own our house and collect rent from the store below. People might think we're better off than them, but we're dealing with many of the same issues other people go through.

Growing up, we're taught that the streets are dangerous and that your home is a refuge. But as I've gotten older, I've realized it's more complicated than that. Sometimes the people who are supposed to protect you end up being the ones that hurt you.

I try to think that it's not happening or just try to ignore it, but I've come to realize that it is a problem and it's affecting my family. But what do you do when you know something has to change? It seems almost impossible to get out of the situation when we are so attached to the ones we love. —Arlet

SAM: A GOOD DAY

It's a good day to go to the park with your family. It feels like one of those days you go out and buy thirty pounds of crawfish and a case of beer and cold drinks chilling in a cooler full of ice. The weather's not too hot, not too cold, with enough wind to fly a kite, and the light from the sun is perfect. I can see my dad and me fishing on the lake, just talking about everything, waiting patiently for a nibble on our line so we could haul back and holler, "I got 'em." I can see my brothers next to us throwing rocks in the water, trying to make them skip, and my mother and sisters feasting off all the crawfish and beer.

Yeah, today would be perfect, but I'm sitting at home on my balcony, trying to block out the voice I hear downstairs slightly interrupting my daydream. I'd ask my parents to take us there, but I already know the answer will be No, or not today, or I have work to do. So I just sit here on my balcony thinking about it.

ARLET: TEENAGE YEARS

Everything's better when you're an innocent child, not knowing the ways of the world, how evil and deceitful people are or how everyone in the world isn't meant for you to get along with or be your friend. Being blinded by all those things made life a whole lot better. It's like a baby who's always happy and smiles, with no problems, worries, or stress at all.

Teenage years are a big deal to everyone. At times, I couldn't understand what everyone was talking about when they'd say, "Oh, they're just going through puberty." It seemed like nothing until it happened to me.

One Sunday at church I went up to the altar and got prayed for by Brother Tim, one of our church ministers. Almost every time someone went to the altar, a minister whispered in their ear. I always wanted to know what they were saying. This particular time, Brother Tim asked me how old I was. When I told him I was twelve, he said he knew something I didn't. He told me this was a time in my life when I would go through rough times. Then he began to pray and I began to think. I decided he might just be right and I joined him in the prayer.

From then on, I waited patiently for the rough times in my life. When they came, I thought I would be ready. I didn't go through the whole going crazy over a boy phase or drug phase. It was nothing of that sort, but I did go through an emotional phase where I felt depressed and sad all the time. No matter what I tried, it wouldn't go away.

SAM: PRIDE AND CONTROL

Some people don't have a father and wish badly that they did. I've grown up with my father, but for years now it's like he doesn't even exist. The retreat began slowly. I noticed my dad seemed to be angry at everyone. After awhile he stopped taking me places almost all together. When I was around him, I tried not to say too much. I didn't want him to get mad if I said the wrong thing.

Sometimes I forget that it's not just us children and our mother. Can you imagine that type of lifestyle? My dad is living with me but still I have to learn to be a man on my own. And when he is home, he's off in Belize. Mentally, anyway. He's always locked up in his room, which is an exact replica of his home country (except for his air conditioner, hardly anyone in Belize has air conditioning.) My dad has a clothes line in his room and still has the hammock.

In Belize anything matches and the same goes for my dad's room. He once had an old orange refrigerator with the freezer built into it in his room. I don't know why, he's different from the average family man.

People in Belize also grow plants. Not your usual house plant for decoration either. Their plants serve a purpose. They grow plants for tea, or pepper plants or coconut, orange, guava or mango trees My dad tried to grow a few of those but they died. The only tree that survived is the Misbelieve with its long dark green leaves and clustered orange fruit the size of cherry tomatoes.

One day I got up enough courage to ask him why he was shutting us out. I asked why he doesn't talk to us anymore. He told me it was because when he talks to us we get an attitude with him. He said he's tired of us talking back and being rude to him. Maybe he was right about us being rude and all that, because we've always been like that with him. Ever since we were young, since we learned how to talk, but he thought it was funny then. He always told us we should speak our mind, but now it became a problem. Now he says we've gone too far. I think that's real messed up. You can't get mad at your children for speaking their minds. We were raised that way.

I hate to admit it but I'm often jealous of my brother Troy. It used to be my dad would wake me up early in the morning to go fishing or help him work doing construction for a few dollars or even just to take a ride. Not anymore. My spot has been filled. I try to get it back sometimes, but I guess my dad doesn't see it.

Despite his distance, I worry that my father has a bigger effect on me than I think. I have problems with pride and control just like him. In fact, a lot of me is like my father. I'm often anti-social and mean to people when I don't feel like talking. I'm even inconsiderate at times just like him. I'm not as bad as him but I can see myself getting closer to the level of negativity he's on. I try my best not to be like him, and still find myself acting almost exactly like him. I can't see how that's possible, but it is. I guess it just kind of grew in me like a weed in a rose bush.

ARLET: THE KEY SITUATION

I can only remember having a key to our house one time. I was thirteen and my dad decided all the oldest children—Ariel, Sam, and I— should have a key. The only time we used our key was when we walked home from school.

We all went to different schools. Ariel was going to McDonogh 35, Sam and I went to St. Paul Lutheran, and Karama, Lisa, and Martin went to Colton. One day Ariel lost her key and borrowed mine. Later on that day, she didn't know where it was.

After awhile, the only one with a key was Martin. If Ariel, Sam, and I got home first we would be locked out. That is so disgusting to be so close to the house and have no way to get in. When I complained about it, my dad said he wasn't making any more keys because we always lost them. I thought to myself, "The place where you make keys is right across the street and it's only a dollar for a new key." Instead of getting keys made, my parents stuck to their usual routine and picked us up from each school we attended.

About two years have passed since then and now all the boys have keys to the house. Sam is the only one with a key to both the gate and the side door to our house in the hallway. There's no telling where they'll end up after school. Usually everyone will meet up at Wicker Elementary where my mom teaches. If they don't, we'll be locked out—even my mama.

One day, Martin and I caught the bus home and the side door was locked and neither of us had a key to the side door. We were locked out for about three or four hours. I was so hot and disgusted, hungry, and I had to use the bathroom. Eventually, I went to sleep on the steps. When I woke up, my mom was nowhere in sight and I felt hopeless. Another two hours passed before she arrived.

The majority of the time, we have to call someone to open the gate for us because we don't have key to get in. Good thing she has a cell phone because we'd be locked out even more.

The key situation is part of a larger problem in our family. Locking things made my dad's job of shutting his family out of his life convenient. But it never failed, whatever he locked we always found a way to break in.

When my dad was mad at my mom, he locked his door so we couldn't get in. When my mom needed shoes and clothes we had to go around and use the key we had to the front door to get into the room. Locking my mom from all the material things didn't phase her; locking her out of his life is what did it for her.

ARLET: CHORES

I.

In my house there's nothing to do but sit down, talk, and eat. Almost every night, all the children go in the kitchen, entering one by one as if someone just called a family meeting. We talk about how Mama always fusses at us when we don't clean up right, saying things like, "How many times you saw me doing that, is that how it looks when I do it?"

II.

I wake with mama shaking me, "Hurry up, go tell Sam to take out the trash, the trash man's downstairs." It's Saturday morning, the one day I don't have church or school to wake up for. It is aggravating to be awake, but not as aggravating as having to smell the trash all weekend.

I go and shake Sam awake in a hurry, cause I can hear the truck getting closer. We go downstairs wearing pajamas and t-shirts, and start moving the heavy bags to the curb. There's nobody on the street, so I'm not too embarrassed of my clothes. The smell of rotting garbage, however, makes me sick.

III.

One weekend afternoon, my mama told me to sweep the kitchen floor. I said okay, but then I stayed where I was to watch the last two videos on 106th and Park. When I finally decided to get up, the number one video of the countdown, "Soldier," from Destiny's Child was still playing in my head. I danced my way to the kitchen, looking around for the broom, as my mama walked in and said, "Didn't I tell you to sweep over an hour ago?" She was exaggerating, as usual.

"Yeah, but I was watching videos and I wanted to see what the top two in the videos was." I found the broom and began to sweep. On the floor was a letter "M" refrigerator magnet left there by my nephew Malcolm. He's always touching something. I also found a clean sock that had been dropped as it was taken out of the washing machine, and one shoe that I have no idea how it got there. I picked up all of the big objects that I didn't want to throw away and gathered all the dirt and dust particles off the floor into a heap. I went in the washroom and to find the dustpan with a brown wooden handle and a turquoise green bottom. It looked as if it was rolled over by an eighteen-wheeler. I wanted to ask what happened to it but it was so funny I didn't care. There was a big long crack that almost divided the dustpan in half.

I didn't know how I could make this work. I handled it very fragile like it would collapse any second and hurried to use it. I put pressure on it so some of the cracks could close and leaned over to the side so the dirt could stay in one as I put even more dirt in it. Picking it up was the hardest part. I got a T-shirt bag and slowly lifted the dustpan up to meet the T-shirt bag so it wouldn't spill all over the floor. Next time I'll use a sheet of paper or a piece of cardboard because that was too much trouble to pick up trash.

ARLET: THE HUMOR OF US

Each person in my house has their own sense of humor. Ariel has loud, wanting to talk about people humor. Sam just give you that look when he thinks something is funny. Martin has dry humor – he will say something and won't think anything of it but to us it's hilarious. Lisa just amens what everybody else says, but adds her own lil anecdotes, laughing so much she can barely breathe. Karama is an old man. He's the type who laughs at his own jokes. Me—what can I say about me?— I'm just a burst of laughter waiting for a joke or rib so I can laugh. My mama sits back, trying to hold a serious face but soon starts laughing as well. My daddy acts so serious. It makes me so mad that he will almost never really laugh— the most he'll do is crack a smile. When he does laugh, he laughs 'til hard tears roll down his face and usually I don't get it.

In my mom's red Suburban, Ariel sits in the passenger side, Sam, Martin, and I on the first row and Karama and Lisa on the last row. One time I saw this big fat lady wearing spandex tights. Every lump, roll, and indentation showed in her leg. "Oh, ya'll look at that lady." Everybody fell out laughing. Ariel said, "Girl, she so wrong for that." Sam, not wanting to say too much, just said, "Why would she put that on?" Martin added, "There's one word for that, ugh." And Karama agreed, "That's too nasty with her fat self." Lisa and I wanted to stop laughing but couldn't. My mama asked, "Why ya'll talking about that lady? Ya'll wrong for that," while trying to hide her smile.

SAM: REPORT CARD

The report card came, and my grades were bad. I was looking at it, talking out loud about how it made no sense even to keep going to school when I was already a year behind, and can't even graduate with Arlet. School was not working for me, and I was ready to quit and try something that would get me somewhere in my life: a job that could provide not only for me, but for my son and Roulette.

As I was talking, Roulette got a mad look and surprised me, "I don't want to be with nobody who ain't trying to do nothing for theyself."

"But I've got a whole year after this one."

"Yeah, but then you've got the rest of your life, and you not going to want to be applying for jobs as a dropout."

I was surprised, but it made sense, and kept me going. I went back to school, and pulled out the grades I needed to get closer to graduation.

ARLET: STRUGGLE

As I lay sleeping in my bed, I can hear my parents in the next room fussing. My heart begins to pound. I'm not sleeping by myself so I wake Ariel to let her know what's going on, partly to be comforted by my sister. We sit up and wonder what's going on. Ariel eventually gets up and peeps through the door and I'm close behind. My dad's face looks like a mad man and my mother looks scared but still staying strong, answering him back, word for word. After a while, Martin, Sam, Lisa, and Karama wake up to a house of screaming and yelling. We all make up our mind that we want to let it be known that we can hear them and please stop.

My dad pays us no mind and slaps my mother in her face. My mother told my daddy, "What did I do to you?" He never answered. We immediately began to cry and yell, "Daddy, stop!" he just kept hitting her. I was so hurt because I thought my daddy loved my mama and yet he wants to make her cry. He tries to make her feel low, calling her stupid and dumb, just all kinds of names to make a person feel belittled. When he was finished we all just help my mama and cried until we fell asleep. From then on, I was scared for my mama and daddy to be alone in a room together because next time we might not be there to stop him.

Ever since then my life has changed. My house has become the place where I get all my negative energy and also where I display my own. There I feel alone like no one understands or no one cares. I feel so tense and build up a wall where no one can get through. I have big issues with trust. It hurts to know that I make others feel bad because of my attitude and I do it so much I don't even know I'm doing it. Sometimes I wonder if this hadn't happened, would I be a better person— the person I long to be?

The last time my daddy hit my mother while we were in the house, Ariel and I were still asleep. I heard my parents fussing, but didn't know where it was coming from. I got out of bed and walked all the way to the back of my house into the kitchen. My mother came out of the bathroom, bleeding and crying. She told us to call the police. At first, I didn't want to because I didn't want my daddy to go to jail. I don't remember who called and let them know what was going on. The police were there in fifteen minutes—, the fastest they've ever come.

My mom had evidently felt like enough was enough. She was in the room packing, not knowing where she was going—just knowing she was leaving. She stopped what she was doing to talk to the police and answered any questions they had. My daddy didn't come down until the police was almost about ready to come get him. When he finally decided to come downstairs we were all waiting. They immediately searched him and put handcuffs on him and read him his rights. Lisa panicked. She was crying like my daddy had just got shot. I stayed strong to calm her down while everyone else was standing in shock. I couldn't believe my daddy was going to jail. He had never been to jail in his life. I felt sorry for him. I also felt sorry for my mama because I knew she was hurt.

To me, my struggle is never ending. I have a hard time trusting males altogether. It makes me think males are out to get what they can from you and send you on your way. Maybe this makes me more realistic. I'm not gullible and I think twice before I trust someone with my feelings.

ARLET:
INTERVIEW WITH MOM, PART II

For a long time I've been wondering what the story was with my mom and dad. I knew bits and pieces but not the whole thing. I wanted to ask, but in a way I felt it wasn't my place to do so. We knew what our mom wanted us to know.

Days at a time, in my mind, I've wondered why she would even consider being with a man who hit her, called her stupid, and who never eased her pain when she was hurt. I would actually cry sometimes when I thought about the way my dad treated my mom and felt that she only stayed because she thought we needed two parents.

Some days he did treat my mom like his wife: he cooked her breakfast and would take her out. Those were the days I felt everything was okay. My mom was safe from getting yelled at, or getting told what to do like she was his child.

Three years ago, in church, I heard my mom tell the story of her physical and mental abuse for the first time. I was heartbroken, hearing what my mother went through and to hear that my dad would do things that were so cruel. Before I heard her speak to the church, I didn't prepare myself, but hopefully you will. The interview starts now.

Arlet: What was it like when you and Daddy were first together?

Emelda: Oh, at first it was nice. I mean, the same way with all relationships: you go through the phases where you get along and you want to be together all the time. He would come on my job to see if I was still there, and when I was getting off. Did you know I was a cosmetologist? I would do hair and stuff like that. I didn't see any signs of him being manipulative or controlling. I guess by being raised with just a mom, I didn't know that men acted a certain way. I didn't expect it.

After I had Ariel, he told me not to go back to work: "I'm gonna pay your bills and everything, don't worry 'bout anything." So I didn't go back even though I wanted to go and I had somebody to watch my baby.

My cousin Marie used to always tell me, "You know, you don't have to get anybody to keep your baby, I'm gonna keep your baby."

After she was born, I didn't go anywhere for months. But when someone asked me if I wanted to go to the skating ring, I said, "Well, I'm gonna go and hang out for a while."

When I got back it was about ten or eleven o'clock at night. The next day I went to him to tell him, "My light bill is due tomorrow."

He was like, "Well, get it from wherever you went skating at."

And I was like, "What?"

"You heard what I said. Wherever you went skating at, just get the money from there."

"What are you talking about? Why are you acting like this?" After that he stopped talking to me for about a week and he wouldn't give me the money, so finally my lights got cut off. I was in the house with the baby crying and by this time it was hot. I'm like, "Man, I'm not gonna let my baby live like this." I packed her diaper bag and I went and dropped his baby off to him. "My baby's not gonna suffer because you want to be mean to me." I don't know who gave me the money to get my lights turned on.

At first, it was upsetting me because I couldn't figure out why he's so angry because I went skating. He finally brought me the money to pay the bill, but I had already paid it. That was the first sign, but then I kept thinking, "Well, I just shouldn't have gone anywhere." Like I did something wrong. And I lived like that for years: afraid to make a mistake or afraid to say anything.

A lot of times, I walked on eggshells. There was a control mindset of a woman's role and a man's role. In his mind, this is what a man is supposed to do and this is what a woman supposed to do. It's not, "Do what I do." It's, "Do what I say." He can go all day and all night, but he has to know where you are. It got to a point [where] I didn't have any prenatal care before Arlet was born. I never went to the doctor. I don't remember leaving out of the house when I was pregnant with Arlet other than to go to the door to let somebody in and let somebody out. I couldn't remember the last time I had gone up and down the steps. It got to the point I didn't want to go up and down the steps. I didn't want to leave out the house. I remember that. And I didn't leave out the house until it was almost time for her to be born.

There was a seventeen-year age spread between us. He never wanted me to work, but he would tell me stuff about his past relationships and said, "They had to work. I wasn't gonna be with no woman that didn't work."

So I was like, "Well, what makes me so different? What makes me so special?"

He was like, 'I don't know." I guess he knew in his heart it was like, "I don't want you exposed to anybody."

S: Yeah, that's what it was. He figured that, you go around other people, they gonna like you, too. He thinks you're gonna talk to somebody else. He doesn't want you around nobody—just stay inside all day and have time for him and nobody else. That's how I am too.

BELIZE

A: What was it like to go to Belize?

E: To see the country? I liked the experience because I like to travel. The first time I went, I enjoyed it because we stayed in an empty house where we didn't have to be bothered with a lot of people. I enjoyed the food. I really liked to eat.

I guess I could say I understood him a little bit better. He was everybody's baby. You know, he was like the golden child when he was coming up, too. He came here so young and accomplished so much at a young age. There was so much poverty in Belize that when he was going back and forth he was almost rich to them. In many places there's no electricity, no indoor plumbing. They still have a cooking shack. With money comes respect and that's a powerful feeling. So I understood why he felt like a big timer when he was here. He owned two or three houses. He had rental property and he worked as a crane operator offshore. He was making a lot of money as a young person.

You know, that's kind of difficult for me because I don't feel like that. I don't care what you have, everybody deserves the same amount of respect. You should treat people kindly, not because of what they have. And they have that mindset bad over there. They were poor, but now a lot of people have a little bit more now—especially his family. His family is one of the affluent families over there. They have people in politics and stuff like that. So, he's looking at all that as a part of him.

His family made me understand some of his ways, but it couldn't explain all of it because a lot of the stuff

that he does here in the United States, he doesn't do that there. It doesn't explain his temper. He doesn't show that side of himself. He doesn't. But when you get back home, he'll remember all that foolishness.

You'll have made up, but when you get home, he thinks about it. Everything is like reward and punishment with him. If you're good and you don't say anything, and you let me do this or that, I'll reward you. But, "If you open your mouth, if you nag me, if you tell me something, then I'm gonna punish you." One of my stepsons heard him telling it to his best friend, "Oh, well, I know how I'm gonna deal with her. She don't have nobody to talk to. I talk to people all day. So for two weeks I ain't gonna say nothing to her. She gonna get her mind right." He'll time it.

After that point—knowing that you're doing this purposely—I stopped letting stuff bother me so much. I started finding people to talk to. He would say, "Well, you ain't got nobody to talk to. Nothin but these kids and they don't know what you're saying anyway. I don't know what you talk to them all day for." Very calculating. You're trying to really mess with my mind. And I was telling him: "Don't play with my intelligence, because I'm not stupid."

PHYSICAL ABUSE

A: Will you talk about the physical abuse?

E: The first time, Ariel was a baby. One of my girlfriends was like, "Let's go have a drink." She was going through something; she was depressed and all of this. So I was like, "Well, I know if I go to another bar it's gonna be drama, so let's just go to ours." When I walked in the bar, it was basically empty. It was just five or six people including Sam, another lady, a guy named Josh, and a man they call Rat. Sam was just acting like I wasn't in there. When I would ask him for anything, he told me no. And you know, I never used to pay for drinks or anything. He was shooting pool with this lady. He was showing her how to shoot shots and standing behind her. By this time I'm ready to go, because I feel like first of all, you're disrespecting me, and second of all, this lady is in here with me. I said, "Well, just give me some money and let me go."

"Man, I'm not giving you nothing."

I said, "All right." I went behind the register, and I hit the register open, I was taking money out the register. He came behind me, grabbed me by my hair, and we actually started fighting in the bar. He had me leaning back over the counter and I remember reaching back and getting a shot glass. And I took the shot glass and I bust him upside the head. Well, now you want it to be over because now you're bleeding, but you punched me in my face and I don't know where it is, but somewhere I got a scar in my face. He told Josh to watch the bar. "I ain't been cut in thirty years."

I left out, and the girl that I was with went and called my mom. I was so mad because then my mom came around there and saw me like that. I went back to my mom's house for two or three weeks. She started working on my nerves, kept telling me about how he was, "I told you this, I told you that." Everyday she reminded me of what happened and made me feel uncomfortable. One day I just got tired of that, because it was like physical abuse here, verbal abuse there. So I said, "Man, I'm just going back to my own house."

That was the first time he apologized. "I'm sorry, and I didn't mean to do that, and this won't happen again." That was the most sincere he had ever been. You know, it would be all right for a little while, and then he would go back to doing the same old things. He would never do anything to the children. He didn't even like me to chastise the children. I kept saying, "Why are you treating me like this?"

"I'm not doing anything! Oh, that's all in your mind." All the relationships he would have: that was all in my mind. I'd catch him kissing on another woman in the barroom—it was all in your mind. To the point where they would come looking for him in the bar. Sometimes I would be in there and they would be so disrespectful "Where Sam at?" But all that was all in my mind. Those were the type of things that would make me leave; and then the fighting.

Right after breakfast he would leave. I would ask him, "Where you going?" "I got a business to take care of. I got a business to run." "I gotta go collect rent" or "I gotta go pick up stock." Once he was gone all day and we would see him passing up and down the Avenue. He would pass me, come in, change clothes, iron his clothes, and leave out. I was like, "Man, we're not staying here." I packed up all the kids. We left and went by my brother-in-law's house. We started playing cards and all the while I'm calling home— he's never answering the phone, so I figured he wasn't home. He had gone out looking for me.

We came home. Everybody had fallen asleep. When he came in the door, I'm thinking he's just coming home for the first time. When he came in the door, he punched me across my face while I was sleeping.

Of course I woke up and he's grabbing me by my hair because I think one of the babies was in the bed with me. He was pulling me out the room by my hair and punching me. He's saying, "Don't you ever have me going around looking for you. I'm riding up and down the street, trying to see where you at, got my kids out all hours of the night."

I remember the kids screaming and hollering. You know, especially Sam. He was trying to pull him off of me. He hollered at them to go back to bed. "Y'all go back in there. Go back in the room. Go back in the room." But of course, they're afraid. Arlet and Ariel are screaming and I'm hollering, trying to get away from him.

The last fight was just so stupid. He wanted to know why I was so attached to one of his little nephews. I couldn't believe it. The last time I left I was like, "I'm not gonna put up with that any more." I called the police and he went to jail. They were falling out, screaming and crying. You would have sworn somebody had done Ariel something, instead of done me something. I just said in my mind, "I'm not gonna let you put your hands on me again." I had in my mind where, if he ever does it again, I'm gonna just kill him in his sleep. It was just that bad.

Ariel was in high school so that wasn't more than about six years ago. And then, you know, I bought a

gun. Probably wouldn't shoot him, because I don't even know how to shoot the thing. But I just got in my mind: I'm not gonna let him do this anymore. The time he went to jail we stayed with my dad for about three months.

GOING BACK TO SCHOOL

A: Why did you decide to go back to school?

E: I always told him I was going back to school. That was a desire that I had, and I wasn't letting anybody take that away from me. The more children that I had, the more I realized that I had to take care of myself. I could have done it with the cosmetology but I didn't want to work hard. It was good money, but it's hard work. A lot of standing, and it's a lot of time away from your family [and] on holidays you have to work extra hard.

He was doing everything he wanted to do. He was taking flying lessons, he started working on the ship—everything he could do to advance himself, he was doing that. I was getting more and more vexed, and more and more depressed. I didn't have the clothes that I needed to wear to look nice when I went places and I was really getting sick of that. I was disgusted with myself, and I was the only person that could do something about it. When he went to Texas A & M for more certification, I talked to him on the phone and I was so serious. "You know what Sam? I need to go back to school. There are things that I want. I didn't just need physical things." I wanted peace of mind that nobody could give me. Nobody's going take care of me the way I can take care of me.

I just stopped being afraid of the threats and stopped putting myself on the backburner for everybody else. I was always last. I was telling him that: I come after your business, I come after your family, I come after your friends, I come after your children—I'm always at the bottom of the totem pole. I need to do something that will make me feel like I'm on the top. After that, it was amazing how things just started falling in place. My aunt got a job at a day care, and I put Karama over there because I knew he would be well-taken care of. I won't have to worry about anybody abusing him. And the same time he started, I registered for school at SUNO.

At first he made it really hard because he didn't want me to study. If I would get up in the morning before everybody else, and I'd be sitting on the side of the bed reading or studying my notes, he would figure I should've been cooking breakfast. "Don't think just cuz you're in school your responsibilities to this house gonna stop." That used to make me so angry. Or, I had to cook before I left and he would watch the kids in those evenings because he wasn't working. And he would come ten minutes before my class started. And I would be calling him, and beeping him and beeping him, and he wouldn't answer the page.

In my African American lit course, I had a professor who I talked to everyday after class. We sometimes met up, and would just sit in one of our cars and talk and talk and talk. I started sharing stuff with her. Once I had a test in her class, and I was twenty minutes late because Sam didn't come back in time. The professor already knew a part of the background story and was like, "If you don't want to take the test today, you could just come back." But I went ahead and took the test and I think, I made an A or B on the test, but I usually had the highest grade

When I graduated, I went to my grandpa's church on Mother's Day. He asked me to come but I didn't know he was going to do a presentation for me. I remember him saying, "Now this girl had to want an education mighty bad, cuz she went back to school with six children, all of em went to different schools, all of em were on time, and she got herself to school on time."

GETTING AWAY

A: When did you first start talking about the problems?

E: I made poor choices. That's how I wound up getting kicked out of college. Literally, failing. Just not going, having fun, stupidity. I just felt like I dealt with a lot of stuff because I made those poor choices, and everybody in my family has a saying, "You make your bed hard you lay hard." I never reached out for help.

I talked to my sister Lisa a lot, but I never went into a lot of depth. She knew I was struggling, and that was the only person that ever tried to really give me relief. You know, just for the sake of giving me relief. My dad would try and tell me about letting the children go off sometimes, and taking them, but I was so attached. I didn't know what to do when I had free time.

I decided one time when they were real little that I was leaving after another incident of physical abuse. At the time, my grandmother's house was empty and we left for months. Sam didn't know where we were. I think Karama was only about two at that time. It was before I started school. When I decided to go back to get my stuff, he had hidden his truck around the corner and I thought he wasn't home. He was waiting to catch me coming home. But he didn't know that even before I arrived, I called the police to meet me there. That kind of shook him up and when I got there, he was crying. I decided the police could leave; I told them I could get my stuff in peace.

I don't think I went back that day, but maybe like a week or two after that I went back. I don't know why I went back.

A: Why is it so hard not to go back?

E: I don't know. That's the million-dollar question. When I moved out, I had peace of mind; I was content. I could come and go like I wanted to. But, I was having a little difficulty with Ariel and then we were starting to have difficulties with Sam in school. His father kept blaming it on me, saying it was my fault. "The family needs to be together" and I'm "breaking up the family"' and I had the kids under stress. And then there were little promises: "We love each other too much, we gonna work this out." It sounds so good at the time. You start thinking about it, "Well, you know, I don't have anybody else in my life. I'm not seeing anybody. It's just empty." And it's not like you need a man to make you feel like a person, but it just was lonely with no companionship.

And then, basically, I feel sorry for him. I really do. Even though he does stupid stuff for no reason; you know, calculated meanness. And it takes a lot of energy to make yourself mean like that. I just feel sorry for him—he doesn't have anybody.

ARLET: SAM'S ROOM

When we were little all my brothers and sisters shared one room. There were two sets of bunk beds and a separate bed for Ariel. But even though we had our own beds, we still all slept with our parents in their room.

I guess Ariel felt that since she was the oldest and there were all these empty rooms in the house, she should get one. I was so excited Ariel got her own room. It was like she was moving out to bigger and better things, even though it was the smallest room in the house and only fit a bed and a reasonably sized dresser. It wasn't all that much better either because at first she didn't even have a door and when she got one, she couldn't lock it. Even though she didn't have a lock, we knew not to barge in whenever we felt like it. When I wanted to enter, I had an already planned out conversation to ease my way in.

Ariel had that room for a couple of years. When she moved out, Sam got that room. Unlike Ariel, he didn't care who came in and we weren't as cautious about entering. We had so much fun in that room. When we got tired, all my brothers and sisters, slept in that room, all in one bed. We all gathered in Sam's room to watch sitcoms on Channel 38 because he didn't have cable. Also we listened to all kinds of music. That room made me feel like we were on our own with no adult supervision.

One day Sam decided he wanted to paint the powder blue walls a darker blue, tile the wooden floors, and paint the shelves white. I was happy because the room felt even more comfortable. Sometimes I went in there to relax and get away from all of the cleaning and arguing.

When his girlfriend moved in, everything began to change. We couldn't just walk in and watch TV, listen to the radio or sleep in there anymore. When we knocked we expected him to open the door, but instead we had to tell him what we wanted or why we needed to come in. Sometimes he acted like he would answer the door, but then he wouldn't. He began to act as if we should know not to knock on his door.

I felt like Sam was pushing us away for an outsider. He rarely left his room, but when he did, he was normal—talking and laughing with us for a minute—and then he would go back to alienating himself from the rest of us. Sometimes he stayed in there for so long, without eating or saying anything, that my mom would tell us to call Sam so she could see what he was doing. In a strange way, it seemed as though he thought his girlfriend was all he had and he knew for a fact that she would be there for him the rest of his life. I wished he would think that way about his family.

SAM: BECOMING A MAN

The process of becoming a man has been a long one. I started getting that feeling about wanting to be grown when I was twelve, and so I started drinking beer and smoking cigarettes. I thought that would make me more of a man. It didn't though— it just made me a kid smoking and drinking.

Then I used to hear older boys talk about sex and having all these girls to do it with. I didn't stop drinking or smoking, but started pursuing more and more girls. By the time I hit fifteen, I had never had sex, but lied about it all of the time to make myself look more mature, and to make me feel like more of a man.

When I turned sixteen, I broke my virgin, and three months later I made my son. I really thought I was grown then, and made sure everybody I knew I had a baby on the way. By the time he was born, I wasn't just a man, I was *the* man. I was living with his mother, working a job, drinking and smoking weed. Yeah, I thought I was the man. Really, though, I wasn't a man. I was a seventeen-year-old boy with more on my plate than I could handle.

A little while after my son was born his mother and I broke up. That's when I met Roulette. At first, it was instant gratification. Then after a while it got kind of rocky, and that's where I am now. I'm in a rocky relationship with a beautiful girl, trying to pursue a better life as quick as possible. I don't want my son to have to wait on me to be a good father.

PART IV: CHANGES OUTSIDE

I've lived on St. Claude, and dealt with the problems associated with it for so long, it seemed like nothing was ever going to change. Sometimes the drama died down for awhile, but then it flared up again.

Around the corner from us in the Bywater, though, white people were moving in and fixing up houses. Slowly, we started to notice that it was effecting our block of St. Claude. We'd see different people walking from around the corner until some of them finally moved in next door. I wondered if more people like them would move in and why they picked the Ninth Ward as a place to live because my family always talked about wanting to leave.

ARLET: NEW PEOPLE ON THE BLOCK

Our block used to be mixed. Our house, our neighbors, the business that's a barber shop now and the church were always black people. The store below our house and the corner store were run by Vietnamese, and the clinic and doctor's office were used by both black and white people. Across the street, black people were always the majority. Around each corner of my house, Piety and Desire were white. Most people were a little older than my dad. There was only one white family that was younger. This family made me realize that white people are not better than my family or any other black family on my block. They only seemed different because they were white. They didn't have a lot of money because their appearance showed it. They caught the bus, and they became victims of circumstance by getting involved in drugs.

Slowly, the white people moved out because of the violence and because so many black people moved there. The whites that did stay did not hold conversations with black people. They kinda kept to themselves—they would just speak and keep going. There was a point and time where I thought white people were almost gone from our neighborhood.

But then I saw a white woman dressed in all black, with big thick Sketcher shoes, long pants, fishnet stockings, and a big book sack and a shaved head. I wondered, "Where is she going dressed like that as hot as it is outside? Is she scared or nervous walking up this block with black boys standing on the block like they owned it?" I started to see more and more white people like this. One day I saw this super tall lady at least 6'2" or something. She had a Mohawk dyed blue, her eyebrows were cut off and drawn back with a blue eyebrow pencil. She was dressed like a punk rocker. I just looked at her and asked, "Why?" I tried not to criticize anyone because of the way they dressed or looked because my teacher explained to me that what is normal to me may not be normal to them. I can't exactly remember what they said, but it was somewhere along that line.

One day a whole bunch of these punk rocker people moved in next door to me. They were really weird to me. They played this accordion late at night like they were celebrating something. They had old stuff in their yard like this old table and chairs they sat around to play their music with a candle or lamp burning. They were really to themselves most of the time. They didn't introduce themselves or even speak at all to us. They boarded up the fence in front of the yard. In front of their house was a big circus looking van. It is very colorful—purple, orange, blue, black and white, with all these little statements written on it. From my brothers' room, I could see lots and lots of books stacked up in one room. I wondered if they once owned a bookstore and kept all the books. They just recently painted their house purple and orange.

Now I'm kind of used to seeing them because there's like five or six who live in that house and around the corner there are more of their kind. Everyday I see someone different.

SAM: CIRCUS PUNKS

Our Piety-side next-door neighbors have always had the same culture. Black people, weed smoking, drug selling: the whole "ghetto" image. But now they're completely different in every way. It's kind of strange seeing white circus punks move in the middle of the hood. It's like everything matches as far as looks, but right there in the middle of the hood is the polar opposite.

These people are the only white people ever, since I was born, to move on St. Claude Street. They dress different— way different— like the type of clothes you wear at a heavy metal concert. Piercings are everywhere. Well, not quiet everywhere but in strange places like in the nose or eyebrow or lip. Their appearance and culture are different, but they're cool people.

When they first moved next door, I would hear people whispering, "Oohh! Look at them people, they look like they just stepped out of a circus!" Some people just giggled to themselves when they passed by, but everybody had a comment or facial gesture.

Not long after they moved in, we started off on the wrong foot. My parents got into an argument with them because they were throwing rocks at our house. We didn't know they were trying to tell us that our dogs were making too much noise with all the barking. So they were mad at all the barking, and my parents were mad at the rock throwing.

Well, that beef didn't last too long. We didn't speak to each other for a while but all that animosity died down. People around my house started accepting them and became close to them. Now everybody knows them as cool people, but nobody really knows them, so I decided to find out what type of life they lived. I was a little nervous about finding out by myself so I asked Abram to join me in an interview with them. I found out a lot of fascinating and wild things about them.

When I first walked into their house, I honestly was scared, real scared. I wasn't afraid of the people or anything, but there was this huge, black, energized dog that kept jumping on me and looking me directly in my eyes. I wanted to jump on a table and yell, but I held it all in.

Besides the dog, the house was filled with books and books, a lot of pictures, and circus stuff. It was still burned in the back room from when there was a fire, but they made it look natural and presentable with all the decorations of pictures and stuff.

This house is a shotgun— everything was straight back. First living room, then bedroom followed by another bedroom, then the kitchen, then the bathroom. We sat down in the middle room. There wasn't an air conditioner but the room was cool. We sat at a wooden table and started the interview. I was especially glad Abram was there since he already knew them. They sold his books, so he was pretty comfortable, and when I saw that, I was a little more relaxed. The interview was going good, but got better when a friend of Tanya's walked in and joined the interview.

SAM:
INTERVIEW WITH TANYA SOLOMON

Sam: Why did you move here?

Tanya: My boyfriend and I were living in New York and we had a project called the Auto-Nomadic Book-mobile. It's that funny looking truck that's parked around the corner right now. [We take it] around the country with a book store in the back that sells small press books like New Mouth from the Dirty South—Abram's got one of these presses—and a little circus show. It was pretty hard to live in New York, because it's really expensive. We were looking for another place to live and we had a lot of friends in New Orleans and we both really liked [it].

I decided to go ahead and buy a house because I had a little bit of inheritance money [that] I had since I was a kid. It was from my grandfather and for family reasons I hadn't been allowed to [spend it] until I found a good way to use it. I never used the money or lived off it and then I convinced my mom that I should buy a house and she was fine with that. [It was] not enough to get a house that has real walls and everything, but enough to get a house like this [one]. I was looking on the internet and that's where you can see every house that's listed for sale and I saw this house. They had actually had this house on E-Bay before. I think somebody tried to buy it and it fell through.

I was staying at a rundown house on Chartres Street between Montegut and Clouet, which is just called

the Clown House where a lot of circus performers stay. That house got evicted pretty soon after.

Abram: What did the clown house get evicted for?

T: This is relevant to this block, too, actually, because these people from California are going around buying properties all around this neighborhood. They're called Delta Properties. The price of property in this neighborhood is going up—what some people call gentrification, other people call real estate development. They are buying a bunch of houses in this neighborhood including that house that is getting painted pink over on Piety Street—you know which one? They've got construction guys in there all the time.

S: Mmhm.

T: They got the Clown House for 18,000 dollars. The house was totally decrepit. It was a mess. When they bought the house, the clowns were evicted. They chopped off the back of the house. It's a tiny double shotgun now and they rent it out for like $800 a side. They make their money back and then sell it really quickly. They've bought a couple of houses on this block, I think.

This house was in the same neighborhood, which is good. I went by the house and thought, "That could be an amazing house." I went to the agent who was selling it and the house was being sold by the Department of Housing and Urban Development. Apparently, this house has had a lot of problems for a long time. We can talk about that. They put a certain price on the house and I offered them a lower price. I prefer not to say what [it] was but let me just say it was really low. It was almost all of what I had inherited, but it was a really cheap house and I got the house.

Beyond having the money to buy the house, we don't really have any money. We can't afford to hire contractors so we're doing all the work ourselves. Okra is an old-time squatter from New York. Do you know what a squatter is?

S: No, I don't. What is that?

T: It can mean a couple of things. In general, it means someone who goes into an abandoned building and lives there. It could mean somebody who just crawls into a building for a couple of days to sleep or—and this happens in New York City a lot more than here but it happens some too— people decide they are going to fix up an abandoned, neglected building and they're going to live there and try to hold it down. Okra had been doing that for a long time in New York City. He's got a lot of con-

structions skills and electric skills, so he's teaching me to do some stuff. That's the reason we're going so slow—we're doing it all ourselves. That's the long answer to your question.

LIVING ON THE AVENUE

S: When did you move to New Orleans?

T: I moved to New Orleans in April 2003. And I bought this house in July 2003. [I] went on Circus tour, came back, moved in here October 2003.

S: Cool. How do you feel about this neighborhood?

T: I really like it. St. Claude is kind of a strange place to be. I'm sure you feel that sometimes, too. But, this is where the house happened to be. I think that Okra and I would not have preferred to live on St. Claude itself because it's so crazy here. I mean, you live right next door, you see everything that goes on.

S: Yeah. I don't like it.

T: Yeah. I like a lot of things about this neighborhood, too. I like that people are really friendly. A lot of people we were friends with before, but we meet a lot of new people all the time. I think we know a lot of people on the block. We don't know you guys so well. I know there was a little bit of trouble last summer. Okra got into a fight with your little brother and I wasn't here when that happened. I talked with your mom and tried to straighten things out.

I think we know most people on the block. Not on the other side of the Avenue but on this side and around the block. We're definitely outsiders here. We're white people, we're from New York. We live a little differently from other people. I guess they would call us like "artists"—that's a catchall term or something. We have strange ideas compared to a lot of people— like the ways we want to make our money and our political ideas and things like that— so we don't always fit in exactly, but people have been very welcoming and we try to be respectful of other people on the block. I thought it was going to be scary all the time living on St. Claude with the crack heads coming by and the people coming from the grocery on the corner, and the drive-bys and all that. But it's not scary at all. We've gotten to know people really well.

S: If you could change anything about this block, what would you change?

T: I would change something a few blocks down. I get the sense that Douglass High School is not very appealing to kids in the neighborhood and that's why kids are hanging out here doing what they're doing—like knowing some of them personally, I know they're really nice kids, a lot of em are really sweet. They're smart kids and I know a lot of them are going to end up spending their lives in jail and they're just doing stuff out on the street and I think if there was something better for them to do. I don't know—you probably know more about this than I do, but I see that they're young. They're probably about your age. You go to another high school. I think that would change the neighborhood a lot.

S: If you had a choice of living in another neighborhood, would you move?

T: I would move right around here, but I would prefer not to live right on St. Claude.

S: Where would you go?

T: Right around the corner. Some place a little quieter, maybe. The traffic makes a lot of noise, too.

S: What other things could make the block better?

T: Well, besides the high school, I haven't really lived here long enough to really know. One thing I would say right off is people should stop throwing their trash down on the ground. I don't think you guys have a yard, but you know, people throw their trash right over our fence. We put trashcans right outside our house, I clean up every couple of days, but it's kind of besides the point because people just use it as a trash can and that makes it look abandoned all over again.

S: Why do you think that's the way it is? The people, the way people act, just the way everything is around here. I mean, it's not known as a good environment to be around and why do you think that is—from your experience so far?

T: Well, my experience here has been pretty brief and I know some things historically about this neighborhood. I know that it used to be a mixed race neighborhood and that when Douglass High School desegregated there was a lot of flight to the suburbs and a lot of houses were abandoned. I would guess, from just reading some history of the neighborhood, that that has a lot to do with the abandonment of the neighborhood. I think a big reason is there aren't a lot of options for the kids that grow up here. But, there's a reason for the positive, too. I think it's very neighborly. I think people know each other. It's not like that in most cities. It's not friendly. You don't see neighbors and go, "How you doing" and all that. And there are some positive things about this block that I can see coming from the outside.

S: What is the best thing about this block and the worst?

T: The best thing about this block—I feel is Gwen. She really holds this block together and she's not afraid to speak her mind when there's something going on.

S: The barbershop lady?

T: She owns the Secret's Salon over here. She's a really, really nice person. She's really loud and funny and can put a light edge on things when things get a little too intense. She's the best thing about this block. The worst thing about this block: I would say the people coming here to buy drugs.

DRUG DEALING

S: It happens everyday. All day.

A: Are you opposed to drugs?

T: Opposed to drugs is a pretty loaded term. I think people should be allowed to do whatever they want to do. I don't think it's the government's business if someone wants to hurt themselves.

One of the things that Okra and I feel strongly about with the drugs—we will not call the police. Unless someone actually comes in here and like attacks us. I got the dog here, I got a baseball bat and whatever, but I don't think the police are helping anybody. I think they're a part of the problem, and they hurt the kids in this neighborhood. If people want to beat themselves up, if they want to hurt themselves, it's their business, not my business. But I'm opposed to the selling out here. I think the kids are falling into a trap that's set for them. I can see why they wouldn't want to go to

a lousy high school, and there aren't a lot of options for them and they might make a lot of quick money, but I think it's really depressing. And I'm opposed to them being out there selling it. On a level of my personal safety, I don't want a bullet coming through my wall. I don't want them having their fights here. The kids themselves are really sweet, but I don't want their skanky customers coming to my house.

S: Are you opposed to people or children?

T: Children using drugs? Selling drugs?

S: Selling?

T: Selling. I think the drug trade is messed up. I think it's a trap for people to fall into. I think it's really depressing to see and I think there's violence that goes with it. I mean, in the one year that I've been in this block, there's been four people killed on this block.

S: Yeah.

T: And most of it has to do with drugs. It's really frightening. It's definitely the worst thing about the block. Yeah, I'm opposed to it but, I don't want to call the police to deal with it. I'd rather deal with it myself. We've tried to tell people one-on-one, "Please do not sell drugs in front of our house." It's not working, obviously. How old are?

S: Eighteen.

T: Has this house been abandoned most of the time you've lived next door?

S: It was never abandoned.

T: Really?

S: They had a whole lot of people moving in, move out, and two months later someone else moving in—always, always.

T: Who do you think was living here? What kind of people?

S: Well, I know what kind of people. I always got a long with the people. I mean, they sold drugs and all that stuff, too.

T: There was a lot of people connected with drugs?

S: Oh, yeah, this was a house for that. The last people that was here had a lot of that going on here.

T: Really? Because the last people that lived here owned the house. They owned the house and still sold drugs out of it. Weird. So this house has always been a drug house.
Why do you think they bothered to buy the house?

S: I don't know. It's a hot spot. You make all your money right here. That's what I think.

T: After we bought the house, we went on a circus tour. We had to cut it short because my dad died and I stayed with my mom for a while in Kansas City, Missouri. I'm not originally from New York. I was in Kansas City for a long time, and Okra came here by himself and opened up the house. I never got to see it when he first came here. There were piles of shit on the floor. There were people coming in the back to do drugs. Gang graffiti. There were just scumbags all around. And we just spent a lot of time removing garbage from the property. I know this house looks like a mess, but it looks a lot better than it used to.

T: So you guys go to school out of this neighborhood and you try to stick to your own. How do you keep yourself out of the nonsense on the block?

S: Man, my parents, they're the whole reason why. They brought us up way different from a lot of these people around here. There are other ways to get money if you want it. They only drink alcohol every once in awhile. I do, too. But we was never raised seeing that kind of stuff unless we go outside. Inside we always had a good example to follow behind. My mama never let us come outside when we was little. And if we did, it was to go to the store my daddy owned downstairs. We always had to go in pairs. Bring your brother or bring your sister.

T: Isn't that frustrating?

S: Yeah, it is.

JAIL

S: Have you ever been to jail?

T: Yes, I have been to jail.

S: Why?

T: I have been to jail for really stupid things. I went to jail this past August for protesting against the Republican Convention in New York.

S: Is it illegal?

T: It is actually not illegal. I was actually standing on the sidewalk at the time, but I spent 39 hours in jail. I've never been in anything but a holding cell. I've never been to jail jail. I went to jail once for having like an equivalent of a garage sale on the street, we call it a tag sale because there's no garages. The police came up and asked if I was selling these clothes and records and I said, "Yeah," and they put handcuffs on me and took me to jail.

S: I don't understand.

T: Let's just say Rudolph Guiliani is a really bad man.

S: Were you scared in jail?

T: I wasn't scared in jail. I was annoyed.

S: I'd be scared.

T: You've probably never been to jail. I hope you never go.

MAGIC

T: Is your dad a magician?

S: Yeah.

T: I thought so. Where does he perform at? Does he do parties?

S: Yeah. He does parties. Anywhere. Sometimes he

pull on the side of the road and he'll start doing it for people. He does all kinds of stuff, too.

T: What does he specialize in? Like card tricks?

S: Beaucoup card tricks, making stuff disappear, people animals, birds. Cutting people in half.

T: So he does full stage illusions. When a tree fell on our house last year, your dad gave us his business card. "Magic Man." [I was thinking], "Hmmm, there's a magician next door, hmmm."

S: It's fun to watch, but I don't think I could do it. I never really asked. Too shy.

T: I don't know how I got on this topic, but you were saying the worst thing.

S: Yeah! We got way off.

DOWNWARDLY MOBILE

A: How do you make your money?

T: I make what little money I make doing food delivery—pizza delivery and food delivery. It's kind of frustrating. I have a really good education and I used to have jobs in publishing. I would say that I'm downwardly mobile.

A: What does downwardly mobile mean to you?

T: Well, I don't know if they use the word yuppie here. But in New York we call people YUPPIES and it means Upwardly Mobile—like, they are trying to move up in the career world, and they're trying to make a lot of money, and get a lot of nice things. I would say that I started out with—not a lot of nice things and a lot of money—but a lot of opportunities and I've gone in different directions from those opportunities.

I have a master's degree in philosophy from The New School in New York, which is the super lefty, European-style university. That's why I'm a pizza deliverer! [laughing]

I don't want to go into too many boring details here, but when you study something like philosophy in the United States usually you have study a lot of logic and math and sentence structure and things like that. [But at the New School], you can study political philosophy, athletic philosophy, philosophy of religion—things that American philosophers usually rule out. Anyway, I have a good education. I used to work in publishing, and then I joined the Circus, and now I do things like deliver food.

A: What's the circus like? Why do you do circus?

T: I was just in love with it. I was pretty old when I started. I had never done any performance before, but there was this small independent circus that came out of this small anarchist publisher called Autonomedia. I had some friends that were involved with that circus and [I heard they] needed someone to go with them and sell books. Basically, the circus was supposed to be a so-called medicine show for the publisher. Do you know what a medicine show is?

S: No.

T: Yeah, it was an old timey sort of thing in the 19th century and the early 20th century. People would make these so-called medicines that were usually alcohol or something worse and put them in bottles and go around the country on a horse and wagon and sell them. They would put on a whole show to sell their crappy products. They would have all kinds of singing and dancing and acrobatics, and magic, and comedy, and that's where a lot of American performance comes from. It was all to sell this product. [This publishing company] thought it would be really funny to sell the books that way. The circus took off on it's own, and they just kept one table selling books at it. I decided to take this book table and turn it into a whole thing on its own.

We traveled. We went off on our own with the bookstore in the back of the truck doing the circus show. Okra had some performance experience and I had gotten a lot of experience with the circus. I'm probably not explaining this really well, because it's probably new concepts. It's also weird thing to anyone who isn't familiar with the independent publishing New Orleans book fair type of theme.

TWO-PERSON CIRCUS

S: You have a circus?

T: Yeah, we do a two person circus show.

S: What do you do?

T: We do things like fire-eating. We did a little bit of magic. Okra's a knife thrower. I don't know if you've ever seen him practicing in the backyard. He's one of the only knife throwers in the United States.

S: Who does the fire eating?

T: Both of us.

S: Wow.

T: Yeah, we did that type of thing. It was a circus sideshow kind of thing. It's not animals and high wire and all that. It was a small circus. We'll get all dressed up in costumes and we have a little stage set and we try to make it funny, so they'll get ready to look at weird books. I haven't done a show in so long; the truck's been broken down.

A: Did you ever get hit with a knife?

T: Yes.

A: Did you ever get hurt bad?

T: I've got scars, yeah.

S: Wow.

T: He only hit me once. He hit me in the thigh. It hurt. We were doing some pretty gross acts like pounding nails from our nose, hanging things from our tongues and stuff.

S: My dad does something like that

T: I bet he does it as a magic trick, but we're doing it for real. Like, I would stick needles in myself.

S: Really?

T: Yeah. Not drug needles. Yeah, walk on broken glass and stuff. It's pretty gross so we try to give it a light edge. The show doesn't get good until a couple of weeks into tour.

S: You ever burn yourself when you eat fire?

T: Yeah, we have accidents all the time, but if you do it right—I bet your dad can use fire.

S: Every time he's always doing something new.

T: I bet he can eat fire, but if you don't do it right, you get hurt. It's not a magic trick in the sense that it's an illusion. You know you doing the thing and you know you're gonna hurt yourself and you also know that it won't kill you and you have certain ways to do it. I'm not going to be responsible for telling you how to eat fire or anything—you got to find out on your own.

S: What kinds of needles do you do?

T: I would do acupuncture needles.

S: What's that?

T: Acupuncture is this Chinese medicine with these long scary looking needles. And I don't want to do things like that anymore to entertain people anymore. I'm tired of grossing people out. I want to do more magic. I'm trying to learn a lot of magic.

We don't make any money from the circus [and] the book mobile. We lose money on it. And the money that we make at our service jobs, a lot of it goes to paying off the debt from that thing. Since the question was how do you make your money. That's how we lose our money. I'm lucky to own this house.

BLACK & WHITE

T: I don't think I'll stay in New Orleans forever, but I'll definitely stay awhile. I'd like to go back to New York someday. I love New York. I just feel at home there. I like the intellectual life that's there. I feel like there are some interesting conversations going on in New York that aren't going on in other places.

S: I've been there before.

A: You've been to New York City?

S: It's tight.

T: It's one of the largest cities in the world. You walk down the street and there are people from all over the world. That's one thing that's weird to me here is that it's all black or white even though there's Vietnamese people who run the store, people don't think about it as different races besides black and white and different ethnicities. It's like you're black or white—it's weird. In New York, it's more broken down.

A: Do you feel like a Jew here?

T: No, I feel like a white person here.

A: Do you feel like a Jew in New York?

T: Yeah, in New York I don't feel like I'm a white person; I feel like I'm a Jewish person. It's more broken [down]. And people are used to other people—like people socialize more with people of other ethnicities that's something that's really weird. There's a black world and a white world and they don't mix much. In New York, you know, your friends would be Chinese, Puerto Rican.

S: Yeah, everybody's so mixed. Everybody. Even my family, they mixed. Japanese people. Spanish people.

T: Is your family from here?

S: Half. I know we have some Indian in us. None of my daddy's family is from down here. He comes from Belize.

T: Belize? Wow.

S: All of em come from Belize and they moved down here because they liked it better.

T: Black here?

S: Well, some of em. But some of em are light, light, light.

T: Everything is pretty much black and white here—there is no other kind of ethnicity that people think about. I mean there are other ethnicities here. Does it seem that way to you? It just seems like everything is either black or white.

PUNKS

A: Or Uptown/Downtown. How are punks different than circus freaks?

T: They're not. There's a lot of cross over between all the strange—and they're not all white, either. But once you are in the circus world, you're in a white [space]. We know a lot of circus freaks that aren't white, either.

The difference between circus folks and punks: there's some cross over and I'd say that has to do with traveling. Punks are people who travel a lot. You'll see them coming through here every fall. They come through New York City in the summer. They tend to wear patchy clothes, have dread locks, they tend not to be terribly clean. They've been traveling on freight trains and they just jumped off the train. There's all different kinds of punks. There are the ones you see in the Quarter who are really kind of rough. I think the punks you see on this block lately are more like artists and circus people who have been traveling on trains. It's probably the way people dress that's the cliché.

A: Were you ever a punk?

T: No, I don't think so. But I know a lot of people who consider themselves punk and travelers.

A: What's a traveler?

T: A traveler is someone who travels a lot but not by airplane and doesn't stay in hotels. It's someone who travels by hitchhiking or riding freight trains or I'll hop in a car and take a ride. They go from city to city looking for adventure. They have friends in different towns. Sometimes they have performances. Sometimes people make zines and distribute them in different towns.

A: How much a part of that world are you?

T: I would say that is my world. That is a big part of the reason I moved here so that I could do that and live at the same time.

T: [to friend] Are you a punk?

Friend: There are so many words that could apply to me. God, I mean, it depends on what you call a punk. Gypsy, punk, crusty, traveler kids, house punk, upper crust cuz I have a cell phone. I'll be talking to a bunch of kids on the street and my cell phone goes off. I guess it depends on who's looking. I wouldn't call myself a punk, but I definitely have hung out with stereotypical punk kids, but also squatters and college kids. I have a kind of colorful background. But I have always been kind of punk, for sure, I've always had that in my heart, but not in the way most people think of it, because I really hate stupid punk kids that just drink all the time.

T: I would say that a definition of punk that also comes back to the first question: why do you want to live here? I don't consider myself a punk. I think it's a really tired word, but for a lot of people who want to find ways to live without being a part of the system, but at the same time not doing things like the kids out[side my house] are doing selling drugs and stuff. People who want to make art, and make their own community projects and things like that. That's called DIY—or "Do It Yourself."

DIY is a word people use at home depot or hardware stores: do it yourself, but it's also used for this kind of stuff. Like, if you don't want to work at a job that means nothing to you and make a lot of money for things you don't really need, um, you can do it more like politically idealistic—um, how would you describe this? I think this is where the cross-over is. Tend not to need such brand new clean things—hence, this house. You get the idea. Living outside the system.

SAM: HACKED UP

I was sitting in my room watching TV with Roulette when my brother Troy called me to come shoot pool with him and my dad. Naturally, I was excited because I never go anywhere with them. While waiting for my sister Chancie to take me, I decided to go outside and smoke a cigarette. While I was in the process of lighting my Kool, I saw about six or seven police cars roll up. One parked on the sidewalk, some in the parking lot, one on the corner and one in front of the barbershop but still in the street, blocking my sister's car.

These police were watching any and everybody who was on the block, and whoever just happened to be walking up the street. They harassed Mario first. They checked him for drugs and a weapon, and asked him a lot of questions about what he was doing outside. After they finished talking, Mario walked off, going towards his house. Then a group of white people who looked like punk rockers walked by. All of them were checked. Three ended up in the back of the car. I think they found drugs. They were sitting in the car like nothing was going on, just talking. They let the rest of them go and they kept walking up St. Claude talking. Then Twine rolled up on his bike to go to the store under my house. He got harassed. They checked him, asked him some questions, then let him go. He went in the store and bought a red juice, then rode off.

The police stayed out there for fifteen minutes just checking people. By the time they left, we didn't even want to go anywhere anymore. We were too scared we might get bothered by the police. We just stayed inside for the rest of the night, watching TV. I was highly disappointed, but I'd rather be in my house than in the back of their car.

ARLET: MR. JAKE

It's dark, and while I'm looking down the street, I see Mr. Jake who lives in the alley near our house. This is the time he usually comes out during the day. He's dressed in his usual khaki pants and shirt, a lime green hat, and a leather jacket. Tanya says he rents out his houses really cheap. Some of them were abandoned when circus performers and artists moved in.

Mr. Jake's taking one small step at a time. His steps are so stiff, like he has to remember how to take another step, but he's moving surprisingly fast. I wonder if he's scared and knows that a lot of people think that he is prejudiced. But with every step he takes, he's calmly smiling.

RENOVATIONS ON ST. CLAUDE AVENUE BETWEEN DESIRE AND GALLIER

SAM: SWIMMING IN THE SEA

I think if I had been raised in a better neighborhood or around more positive people I wouldn't have so many problems. Not that my parents didn't do a good job raising me, it's just the sea I'm swimming in. From the Avenue to my school, the police are casting their nets—looking for people to fill up the jails. It is easy for me to be caught. I have already started to deal with the courts and paying money for people to stay out of jail.

See, the whole system is like a big net, and the Ninth Ward is where they do a lot of fishing. The net is not concerned whether they catch a good or bad fish. And me, I am just in the water. It's where I was raised, so a lot of the time I can't help or avoid being caught up. Just riding up the street is taking a chance for me: a young black man driving a car. The police have pulled me over and acted as though I had stolen the car. Sometimes I have this sinking feeling that no matter how much I struggle to get free, I'll never be able to get free as long as I'm living where I'm living.

Getting out is way harder than staying in. I feel like I'm in a river, trying to swim upstream, trying my best and my hardest to avoid problems. Roulette isn't making anything better for me. I mean, as far as motivation, having my back, and telling me to never give up—all that stuff is cool. But she's swimming in the same sea. She's gotten kicked out of John Mac and has managed to get caught up in the net. Now we have to pay into the courts and waste our money on bail.

Being with her is exactly what her name is: "Roulette," a game of chance. Some days it feels more like Russian Roulette, because she brings heavy duty drama into our lives. Sometimes I am sure it will end up with me in jail or dead. I'm taking that chance by being with her. All of this is part of the sea I'm swimming in, and it's rough, dangerous, and deep.

PART V: MOVING OUT

It finally happened. My mother finally gained enough frustration, anger, pain, stress, and strength to leave the house. My dad locked her out, and that was the straw that broke the camel's back. Since that night, she's never seen the inside of that house.

I'm glad for her and the rest of my brothers and sisters. Now they don't have to deal with my dad stressing their brains.

It's good that they left. It puts everyone in a better situation. Now my mom can do what she wants without having to deal with however he feels about it. My other siblings don't have to deal with my dad starting huge arguments over nonsense. My dad doesn't have to worry about the bills being so high, and I don't have to deal with all the arguments and hearing gossip about my girlfriend every time her name comes up.

I always looked at other people's families who were broken up and wondered how they were dealing with something as bad as a split up home. Now I see for myself. I never thought my family would actually break up. Sometimes I still can't believe this situation. Sometimes I'm just like, "Wow, they're really gone." I know that my mom was under a lot of stress when she left, and moving helped release some of it, but I wonder if she has any regrets. I wonder if my dad misses her and the rest of my siblings at all.

I really can't say that I'm hurt, or sad, or angry because this isn't the first time we split up and I'm sort of used to it. But overall, I do believe this was the final episode of my family's togetherness. It's really officially over, and will never be how it was when we were young. Yes, there have been times when my mother left before, but I've always had a feeling we were going to go back. This time it feels like she's gone for good and will never look back at the place she left. And to be honest, I can't say I blame her. I wouldn't want to be with someone who treated me bad and physically hurt me. —Sam

ARLET: GLADIOLUS STREET

The stress of living on St. Claude is over. Now I can come home to a more peaceful environment: no yelling about the bills, no worries about if someone comes over will my dad get a nasty attitude, or am I going to have to stop my dad from hitting my mom.

Living on Gladiolus is a big turn around from St. Claude Avenue. Now I leave in a "real" neighborhood, with houses and cars in the driveway, kids in the street playing double dutch and riding bikes, and tossing a football from one end of the block to the next. I can sit in the front yard and not hear, "Come here bitch," or a mother telling her child, "Walk your stupid ass up." On St. Claude people are around all hours of the night. Where I am now the streets are cleared at nine o'clock

There used to be days when I didn't want to go home, because I knew home would put my mom in a bad mood. Our new house has put her in a more happy-go-lucky mood with us, and she doesn't come down as hard as she used to because no one's there to tell her what she needs to do and what is not getting done.

We all moved with my mom, even Ariel, who just got honorably discharged from the Air Force. But Sam stayed on St. Claude with my dad.

Still, there's a lot of things I miss about St. Claude. For one, having a store right downstairs. I especially miss the relationships I had built with the Vietnamese people who run the store. The thing I miss most of all about St. Claude, though, is the people I've grown up with—the way they made me laugh when I was in a bad mood. I miss the conversations I had with Twine about school and how our lives would be in the future. I miss Lemon asking me when I was going to be his girlfriend and talking with Keith about any and everything, but especially music. I miss the random interactions on the Avenue, like when a man would pass singing, "Baby when I used to love you" or when someone would call out to me, "Hey sweetie. You see this man? He's a gentlemen." When I sit out on my porch on Gladiolus, I barely have anyone to talk with and I rarely see people my age. Despite all the things I miss about St. Claude Avenue, I don't think I can go back.

SAM: DECIDING TO STAY

I decided to stay and am glad to say I did. One thing I learned about my dad is you get out what you put in, with interest. Now, you know, I've talked about how he hardly spoke to us or he only spoke when there was a problem. I hated that. I hated that a lot, so I decide to do something about it. Since he didn't speak to us, I started speaking to him.

I didn't start getting the results I wanted all at once—it took a good bit of time— but I eventually did. After a while, I got comfortable with how close we'd gotten. It felt like when I was younger. I knew if I left with my mother, all the time it took for us to be close again would die out after a while—a short while—and I didn't want that to be. I've always liked being around my dad. I like driving from place to place with him all the time and asking a million and one questions.

I do often wonder what my mom and my other siblings are doing. They probably have company every day and have a lot of fun doing just about whatever they want.

My little brother Karama's probably arguing with everybody else—he can be aggravating sometimes. I see my mother waking everybody up for school. I picture her being angry with somebody almost every morning for making her late for work.

Above all, I see more freedom and relief for my mother. There will still be a little stress and a few problems, but I see her handling things better on her own.

SAM: TROY

It was cool while it lasted—it was all good—but now he went to Chicago to live with his mother. Things weren't going the way it was supposed to be with him, so he saw it was fit to leave. Honestly, I wish that he could have, or would have, stayed.

When Troy first moved here, he wasn't much of a role model for me. Not that he was a bad person or anything, because he wasn't, but he was never home. He was always gone with my father, which made me kind of jealous.

Eventually, I started going with them too. When I did, he talked to me about life— what I should and shouldn't do to be successful. He perfectly played the role of a big brother. He always told me how I should save my money, and how to deal with problems like fights or arguments. He told me to never fully let my guard down, or fully trust girls. He said if I trust a girl too much, I will hurt really, really bad if I ever find out she is cheating. He said not all of them were like that, but 90-95% were all cheaters, and it will be really hard to find a girl who is really dedicated. He talked to me about drinking responsibly, and how I shouldn't smoke cigarettes. Yes, I've heard it before from my parents, but who listens to them about things like that?

He left because he got on bad terms with my dad, just like I once was, but unlike me, he didn't suck up

or try as hard to get back close like I did. He just left and got on with his life, which might be a plus for him, but is a loss for me.

Now, once again, I have to look up to myself. He said he didn't know when he was coming back. He said it may be years and years from now, but I hope it won't be that long. My guess is that he'll be back when he's stable enough to support himself and get an apartment. But by that time I'll probably have my own home, too, and won't really need a big brother to coach me on life.

GRADUATION

I've heard my dad just recently left to visit Belize. It's not surprising that I had to hear about it instead of him telling us himself. I can't say I'm saddened that he's gone because when he was here, I didn't see or speak to him. It feels like a long time ago that we used to go fishing together or riding around "taking care of business." When I was young, wherever my dad went, I wanted to go and half the time he took me. If I wanted something or something wasn't going my way, all I had to do is go to my daddy and he did whatever he could to make it better.

But over the years, as he retreated, he began to make a bigger and bigger miration over any thing I asked him to do. It's come to this point where I feel like I'm through. I'm not worried about asking anymore. He knows that and now he doesn't make it his business to voluntarily give us anything.

Today, this distance exists between us, which is why I was surprised that I had mixed feelings about my graduation. That's a time in his life when he should feel proud of me and recognize that the things that he instilled in me were not in vain. He always told us, "One thing I want you all to do is get your education." If he didn't talk to me at all that day, I would have been okay—just him being there was what I wanted. I wonder if he would have come if I had asked. I wonder how he feels about missing this really big moment in my life and does he have any regrets at all.

When I saw he wasn't in the audience, I thought about how through all my dad's mishaps and disappointing times, my mom has been there to try and take up his slack. My mom mentioned one time she loved us "in spite of" not "because of" and I knew from then on that no matter how mad we make her, she will be there. And she always is.

Despite what I feel all I can think now is: I made it. I made my way through high school. The hard part is still to come: now I have to get through college.

ARLET & SAM:
INTERVIEW WITH MOM, PART III

During all the times when my mom left my dad, she never told us how she was feeling. Although I could never understand why she went back, it just felt like something she was used to do doing. At the end of the writing this book, my mom had left my dad again and I wanted to know how she felt about it. Sam and I also wanted to know how she felt about us sharing our family's story.

Arlet: This time do you think you're going to be able to stay gone?

Emelda: I think so. I know I care about him. I really, really care about him. I just don't like the way he makes me feel now. The more I work, and the more I do, the worse you make me feel about myself. I don't like the money issues. As soon as I started working, everything was about money, money, money. "You don't help pay no bills around here. You don't do this, and you don't do that."

I don't want to go back to feeling or thinking that I'm not worth much—that I have little value—because I feel like I have a lot to give

I'm sick of the obligations, too. I'm really tired of being a responsible person—for you, and for your welfare, and for the house and for the cooking and all of that until I just basically shut down. Now, I rarely cook because I don't have the energy. I don't

have the stamina for it. I just don't want to be in a relationship anymore.

I'm to the point now where I'm really tired and it's affecting my health. It's not just affecting my mental wellbeing; it's affecting my physical wellbeing. I have to take care of myself. I'm losing too much weight [and] my hair is falling out in spots. It's too much stress for me and my sugar level is going up. I'm to the point I don't want to eat. Um. And I feel like because of the stress, I engage in a lot of what I call self-destructive behavior. It may not seem like it to other people, but to me it's self-destructive. I always want something to drink. I used to smoke one pack of cigarettes a week. Now I might smoke three packs of cigarettes in a week. When he walks in the room, I need a cigarette.

It's affecting me to the point that I don't ever want to go home. Dealing with little children at work can be draining. But not knowing that you can't ever go home and lay your head down and rest, or have some peace because you're afraid of never being able to sit down.

MOURNING

I guess it hurts too much this time. It really hurts too much. It's really sore. And sometimes I feel like any minute I'm about to crack. I'm starting to notice I'm sensitive to every little thing. If I see somebody without a mom and a dad, I'm sensitive about that. Or I notice every bad child in the school, because sometimes teachers are cruel to those kids too.

It's like a lost feeling. I keep saying I want to write him a letter and just let him know: "I've always thought that if I ever left, I would leave because we just didn't love each other any more. But this is not the case. I still love you. And in spite of all of that, I still can remember some of the good stuff that we did – I could still remember the good qualities that you have – that you choose not to let come through. You choose it because you trying to control my mind. And if you didn't try to control the way that I think, what I did, where I went, it would be much better. But you punish people too much. You are vengeful and I don't like that.

I don't want to ever be in a position where you have so much control over me that you don't even give me a key to the house or that you lock me out. One o'clock in the morning, you're unplugging phones so I can't call anybody, you're locking doors so I can't get in. I don't want to live like that."

I'm afraid that if I ever go back, he's going to do the same thing. The lies are not going work this time. You're just going to repeat the pattern. Every Easter, I think about the sufferings of Christ and I get real, real emotional. Around that time I always feel this burden. This great, great sadness. Even though I know about the resurrection, I feel like somebody died. That's how I feel right now. I couldn't explain it, I couldn't put it into words, but now I know what it is. It's like somebody died. And man, that's what it feels like.

Rachel: There's a mourning that happens around Easter, even though there's this resurrection afterward, and I was just thinking of the amazing metaphor that there will be——

E: Some glory. Yeah.

ARLET AND SAM

A: What is your relationship with me?

E: We have a very close relationship. Sometimes I think it's unnaturally close because she feels mostly everything I feel. With all of them I feel this bond that's unique. But the different bond with Arlet is that she will take care of me without fear. If anything is wrong with me, she would sleep on the floor by my bed. She nurtures me more than the other children.

A: Well, that's something nice to hear.

E: Sam and I have a strange kind of closeness too. It's like on the down low kind of close, because nobody knows the conversations we have, how we talk real sometimes – for no reason. We are just sitting in the room with each other, and one thing leads to the next, and before you know it we're in a deep conversation – I mean real deep, you know, emotionally, spiritually, all kinds of ways. I used to tell him all the time, "You're a good boy, you're a good son, stay good." I don't know how long that's gonna last. But the thing about it is, he doesn't have a problem telling me he's sorry.

I'm really proud of Sam. There are a lot of obstacles and a lot of hurdles if you got to stay in the environment that he grew up in. There are a lot of things he could've done and could be. And he doesn't realize the inner strength that he has that kept him from doing a lot of those things when it wasn't popular. He's still struggling and striving, you know, to get his education, and I just hope that he will realize the potential that he has to do something great. I wish he would channel more energy into himself than other people. And sometimes I have to tell him, "Don't worry about me." I know that he thinks about me a lot. I know he tries to hide it when he makes decisions that he knows I'm not going to be proud of, because he doesn't want me to be disappointed

WRITING OUR STORY

A: What is it like for us to be working on this book?

E: When I think about them, and I think about the book, it's just overwhelming pride that I feel. I hope that it makes them feel better about themselves. Maybe you don't feel so frustrated because now somebody knows your story and somebody knows your struggle. And it's inspiring because you're still standing. And you did not have to resort to some of the stuff that other people say they resorted to that lived in similar situations.

A: And I think a lot of people think we have the perfect life. You think that ma?

E: There are people that envy our family; they envy the relationship that I have with my kids. I don't know why but people we don't know will see us interacting, and they are like, "Wow, you're really close with your kids." And that's just like second nature.

I was so hard on them. I did not want them to be like everybody else. And the stuff that we did was to let you know, you don't need outside influences. We have each other. That was how I was raised: we had each other. Our house is the house everybody flocks to. We can't get rid of people, but we like it and people feel comfortable and they feel homey around us. They don't know the struggle. But it's the attitude. It's not what you go through, it's the attitude that you have while you go through it.

Sam: It's how you carry yourself.

E: I'm not going to allow everybody to have this mopey spirit, because I'm not going have this mopey spirit. That's number one. And I realized that early on, when I used to be down and went through a phase of depression, that I didn't ever want my children to experience that! That's why I know I got to get them out of this because they're talking about it too much. They're talking about how it affects them. Before it was unspoken; nobody said too much about it in the house.

S: I was just about to say if we were to carry ourselves the way that we feel, then people wouldn't want to be around us, because who wants to be around somebody who's miserable all day?

E: I used to be miserable, just bad. But it was like a silent suffering because they didn't know. Everyday, I'm just mama. "Mom, I'm ready to eat. Mom I want some cookies. Mom, can I have a cold drink? Ma, can I have a pie? Ma, can I have a pickle? I need to go here." Sometimes I try to explain it to them: "You don't understand how deep I feel about some things." But, when I looked at their writing, it made me more sensitive— a lot more—to how they're probably feeling too.

A: At first, I didn't even think it was important to write about. I thought it was just a way of life. I thought it was the same for everybody, but a lot of what we do is different from everybody else. To me, that's what made me want to write the book even more.

S: It helped me get a lot of my feelings out. When I talk, I can't really express how I feel as much as when I write. I can show people better how I feel about certain situations and when people read it or go over it, I can express myself better.

A: What do you see in your future about two years from now?

E: About two years? I hope to be certified in early childhood and special ed and I want to work on my Masters in social work.

A: Two years from now, where do you see us?

E: Hopefully I'll see you in college somewhere with a little part time job, and Sam in college and a little part time job.

A: That's a lot.

E: Other people have done it. You can do it too. It ain't gonna kill you. I hope two years from now we'll be healthier. More— how can I say it—normal. But, I don't feel like we're so abnormal, it's just that our problems are different than other people's.

REST IN PEACE TWINE

It was looking like life was about to deal us a happy ending. My mom's built a safer home for us away from the Ave. But even as far away as Gladiolus Street, the news came. It's too much to swallow. I still can't believe it—it's just unreal.

One of the most important people in my life, who I felt the closest to, was murdered just before we went to press. I feel a hurt I never felt before. It's all bottled up inside and waiting to be released one way or another.

Twine was a person who was full of positivity. He wanted everyone to get along and stop the hate. He had goals and aspirations in life that won't be achieved.

People say, "God makes no mistakes," but this wasn't a mistake—it was done by someone. There's nothing you can say to make me understand why.
—Arlet

THE NEIGHBORHOOD STORY PROJECT
OUR STORIES TOLD BY US

What you have just read is one of the five books to come from the first year of the Neighborhood Story Project. This has been an incredible year for us, and we thank you for your support and attention.

The Neighborhood Story Project would like to give a big shout out to the people of the City of New Orleans—y'all are the best. Thank you for showing so much love.

There are lots of folks and organizations that have made this possible. You have come through with stories, with food, with love, and with money—and believe us when we say that all four are necessary.

First off, we'd like to acknowledge our great partners, the Literacy Alliance of Greater New Orleans and the University of New Orleans. Specifically, Peg Reese, Rachel Nicolosi, Rick Barton, Tim Joder, Bob Cashner, Susan Krantz and Jeffrey Ehrenreich have been excellent supervisors and colleagues.

To Steve Gleason and Josselyn Miller at the One Sweet World Foundation. Thank-you for getting this project from the very beginning, and for having such awesome follow through.

To the institutions of the city that have been good to us—thank you. Good institutions play such an important role in making a place. Specifically we'd like to thank the Greater New Orleans Foundation, The Lupin Foundation, The Louisiana Endowment for the Humanities, Tulane Service Learning, The Schweser Family Foundation, and the guys from the Cultivating Community Program for donating the proceeds from your work with Longue Vue to help us get these books out.

To all of the individuals who have stepped up and given so much—from the donation of stamps to all the folks who have trusted us with their money. To Phyllis Sassoon and Mick Abraham for donating their cars. To all the folks who contributed, from the change jars at Whole Foods to the checks and food donations.

Thanks to our incredible steering committee, GK Darby, Peter Cook, Norbert Estrella, Tim Lupin, and Eliza Wells.

To Kalamu ya Salaam and Jim Randels at SAC, for taking us in and showing us the ropes, and giving us support as we try to grow. If we have done anything right as teachers it is because you have taught us.

To the administration of John McDonogh Senior High, Principal Spencer, and the past principals Winfield and Goodwin, thank you for being such great partners. To Ms. Pratcher and Ms. Tuckerson, thank you and bless you for dealing with all the head-

110

aches we cause. And to the staff at John McDonogh, we are so proud to be working with you.

To Elena Reeves and Kenneth Robin at the Tchopshop, thanks for being great designers, and for being such great sports about working with us. And to Jenny LeBlanc and Kyle Bravo at Hot Iron Press, thank you for being great designers/printer and for moving to town.

To Lauren Schug and Heather Booth, for transcribing and transcribing, above and beyond the call of duty.

To Anita Yesho for copy editing at short notice.

To Stephanie Oberhoff, and Communities in Schools- your mission is beautiful and your execution is great.

To Beverly McKenna, thank you for giving us such a beautiful office when we were only a sliver of an idea.

To Gareth Breunlin, who laid out the books and designed the covers. You have made our ideas come out on paper in a way that has honored all of the work and love involved.

To Davey and Jamie for being our dogs.

To Jerry for grant-writing, copy-editing, and being our hero.

To Dan, for his constant input, sharing a car and a computer, writing grants and cooking numerous dinners for the NSP.

To Shana, for promoting this project like it was your own, and for the input and help and grace.

And our biggest thank-you and respect to all of the Bolding, Jackson, Nelson, Price, and Wylie families. Without your love and care, this would not have been possible. Thank you for believing in the project and the work, and for making these books what they are.

And to Palmyra, Lafitte, St. Claude, Dorgenois (and the rest of Ebony's Sixth Ward), and N. Miro, thank you for your stories. We hope you like the books as much we liked making them.

The list is so long because so many of you have contributed.

Thanks for reading.

For the Neighborhood Story Project

Rachel Breunlin
Abram Himelstein

P.S. Thank-you to Richard Nash, Ammi Emergency and Soft Skull Press for believing in us and New Orleans in our time of need.